THE SUPREME GODHEAD

CHRIST

The Corner-Stone of Christianity.

BY

WILLIAM R. GORDON, D.D.

SECOND EDITION, REVISED AND ENLARGED.

NEW-YORK:
BOARD OF PUBLICATION
OF THE
REFORMED PROTESTANT DUTCH CHURCH,
337 BROADWAY.

1855.

John A. Gray,
PRINTER AND STEREOTYPER,
95 & 97 Cliff, cor. Frankfort.

PREFACE.

This small volume was published six years ago. The author has received repeated applications for another edition, and in compliance with written and verbal requests, now reïssues it, differently arranged and somewhat enlarged. He has abridged some arguments, omitted others for substitutes, more directly coming under the general heads of the discussion as here presented, expanded some, and added new matter; but not seriously to affect the original design of "multum in parvo." In its present revised form, he thinks it will be more acceptable to his readers, because presenting more prominently the peculiarity of discussion he deems of importance, in this all-important controversy.

The opponents of the Divinity of Christ, are ever appealing to Reason. The drift of their writings is to show, that the advocates of this doctrine have "most uncommon skulls;" that the imbecility, irrationality, irrelevancy, incompatibility, inanity, absurdity, etc., of our arguments, really impeach us before the tribunal of Reason; that our doctrine is contraband by the laws of common-sense; and impracticable to a philosophic faith. Just here, are we ready for defense; prepared to show, that as they professedly *admit* the veracity of the writers of the Bible, their faith places them in a wilderness of dilemmas, all of vigorous growth from the soil of Reason. And if it can be done, they can have no reasonable objection that,

> Each strong dilemma, in its turn and place,
> Shall show their system in a desperate case.

At the same time, we disavow all intention to place them in any thing like a false position. The subject is too serious, and the interests of truth too weighty, to allow any such attempt, had we the disposition to be unfair in this respect. Our aim is to convince by well-founded argument, by assuming the very ground which we have often been represented as avoiding, and by pursuing a line of discussion with which they ought to be the last to find fault, who deal in *logical* expedients, to overwhelm our view of truth with an avalanche from the lofty summit of human reason. Taking our turn in this way, we sincerely hope may not be a matter of complaint to any of our readers, who may bestow reflection upon what has here been presented.

A writer, who has given a very lucid account of the system we oppose, informs us, that "Unitarians take the Bible in their hands, and sit down to read it, as plain unlettered Christians, and with prayer for divine illumination." We feel quite sure such is the most likely way of arriving at the truth; and for this very class of minds, disposed to receive the truth, with the simplicity and honesty of little children, from the sacred page, we write. We wish to show that our doctrine is fairly deducible from plain statements of Revelation, and that the admission of its opposite is incompatible with the reception of the Bible, as a rule of faith and practice; because the faith it enjoins and the practice it inculcates require us, as we think, to receive the Lord Jesus Christ, as an *original* Being, uniting two natures in one person, the divine and the human, to effect the great purpose of our redemption. We think it quite unwise, *à priori*, to limit God, by saying this involves an impossibility; it is assuming the very thing to be proved. Now, if we take the Bible and "read it as plain unlettered Christians," and find *two* classes of didactic affirmations teaching us that Christ is both God and man; and if it involve no intrinsic absurdity, should God please to form such a union for a specific purpose, why should our doctrine be "a stumbling-block" or "foolishness" to any man, thus actuated by a sincere desire to know what directions are given in the way of elucidating the *answer* to that question, "What must I do to be saved?"

The mode of proving the divinity of Christ is the same employed to prove the divinity of the Father. It can be done in no other way. The arguments in the one case, from the Scriptures, are the same as in the other; and they are equally conclusive. They are *positive*, and can never be answered by *negative* ones. If we prove that Christ is *God*, that proposition is not disproved by the evidence that he is *man*.

The system we oppose is *Socinianism*. But although we prefer to call things by their right names, lest the use of this term should prove offensive, we have taken another as a matter of convenience, namely, *Unitarianism;* because it has been appropriated by the largest Body denying the divinity of our Lord, and is now by common consent understood to designate all who repudiate this point of Christian faith. We use it, however, under protest; for the writer, and all those who think with him, are in the strictest sense Unitarians, as they most firmly believe in the unity of God, and in the subordinate relation of Jesus Christ, as Messiah, Mediator, and Man, to the Father. Hence we yield that to which they are not exclusively entitled.

But there are other Bodies, besides the one referred to, who embrace Socinian doctrine, and are not ecclesiastically known by the term Unitarian, namely, *Christians*. One of their writers says in the history of this Sect: "With very few exceptions, they are not Trinitarians, averring that they can neither find the word nor the doctrine in the Bible. They believe 'the Lord, our Jehovah, is *one* Lord and purely *one*.' That 'Jesus Christ is the only begotten Son of God.' That the Holy Ghost is that divine unction with which our Saviour was anointed, the effusion that was poured out on the day of Pentecost; and that it is a divine emanation of God by which he exerts an energy or influence on rational minds. While they believe that Jesus Christ is the Son of God, they are not Socinians or Humanitarians. Their prevailing belief is, that Jesus Christ existed with the Father before all worlds." In other words, they are *Arians*.*

Friends, (Hicksites.) One of this Body thus writes: "We believe in the divinity of Christ—a divinity not self-existing and independent, but derived from the Father, being the Holy Spirit, or God in Christ."†

Restorationists. "In relation to the *trinity*, *atonement* and *free will*, the Restorationists' views harmonize with those of the Unitarians."‡

Universalists. "Very generally, Universalists have come to entertain, what are commonly called Unitarian views of God, of Christ, of the Holy Spirit, and of Atonement: at least there appears to be a very general similarity between us and the English Unitarians, not only on those subjects, but also on the nature and duration of punishment, on the subject of the devil," etc.§

* Rupp's History of Religious Denominations, (1844,) p. 169.

† Idem, p. 328. ‡ Rupp's History, p. 655. § Rupp, p. 730.

From these extracts, it will be seen that our system is opposed to Arianism and Socinianism, each of which embodies the great characteristic of Unitarianism, as thus expressed by one of their writers: "Unitarians maintain that God is one mind, one person, one undivided being; that the Father alone is entitled to be called God in the highest sense; that he alone possesses the attributes of infinite, underived divinity, and is the only proper object of supreme worship and love. They believe that Jesus Christ is a distinct Being from him, and possesses only derived attributes; that he is not the Supreme God himself, but his Son." "This must be the great leading doctrine, the distinguishing, and, properly speaking, the only distinguishing feature of Unitarianism,"* namely, the *negative* doctrine, that Christ is not the Supreme God. Inasmuch as we aim to specify all these Sects as involved in the same fatal error, the *term* we use, must be understood to include all, though it expresses a doctrine peculiar to neither. We use it, as has been said, for the sake of convenience, and to save circumlocution; and respectfully ask all of them, candidly to consider whether reason and consistency do not require them to accept our doctrine, or reject the Bible, and thus become Deists? Because we think they can not, will not do the latter, we hope some at least will do the former, "that they may find mercy of the Lord in that day."

* Rupp's History, p. 704.

INTRODUCTION.

To those who believe that the Bible contains the will of God for the guidance of Man, the following observations, preliminary to the argument presented, must appear self-evidently true.

Our title-page expresses the doctrine which we intend to demonstrate not only by direct proof, but by the *consequences* that fairly flow from its denial; and we think no exception can be taken to this manner of handling the subject. In our judgment, the argument technically called REDUCTIO AD ABSURDUM, is eminently fitted to convince men of the truth of this doctrine. It has the advantage of a constant appeal to first principles, and to common-sense; and is the shortest way of screwing up the mind to a permanent decision. The greatest respect for those who differ from us, is perfectly compatible with our anxiety to convince them of what we think dangerous errors; nay, the very attempt to lead them to what we are persuaded is the truth, if fairly interpreted, will secure for us a hearing.

Our appeal is to REASON, and we address our argument only to those who can reason, who dare reason, and who will reason. We have somewhere read: "He who can not reason, is a fool; he who dare not reason, is a coward; and he who will not reason, is

1*

a knave." This is brief. It describes those to whom books are of no use, and for whom they were never intended; and if any such happen to get hold of this, we hope they will quietly lay it down. It is written only for reasonable men, who are willing, irrespective of sects and parties, to have their opinions sifted by the FAN of Bible truth. If their opinions stand this test, it will be to them a matter of rejoicing, a solace and source of peace. If they do not, the sooner they are abandoned the better.

Because salvation is a matter of mere mercy, and not of justice, God has a right to settle the grant according to his own good pleasure. He has a right to prescribe to sinners what they *must believe*, as well as what they *must do*. The DOCTRINES of the Gospel are therefore authoritatively given for this express purpose, namely, to form our system of religious belief, and to regulate our course of moral action. Were salvation to us a reward of works, it would be connected consequentially with our course of moral action; but because it is a gift of grace, it is suspended upon our system of religious belief. We therefore can no more arbitrate in matters of faith, than in matters of morals; and we are just as responsible for our faith as we are for our practice. Were this not the case, the solemn declaration would never have been made: "He that believeth, shall be saved: he that believeth not shall be damned."

That salvation must be consequent upon a right faith, and independent of human merit, is obvious from God's method of estimating character. His rule is this: "*As a man* THINKETH *in his heart,* so *is he.*" Now if we pursue a course of right acting in matters of mere moral conduct, and yet a course of wrong thinking in matters of religious belief, it is of no moment how commendable our external lives may be, we can not bear measurement by this rule; and being found wanting, we can not meet with the mercy of our Maker for this simple reason; instead of obeying his prescriptive will, we set up a standard of our own he can never acknowledge, and thus become guilty of an act of the highest rebellion.

All doctrines are not alike important. All errors of faith are not alike prejudicial to the welfare of the soul. But some doctrines are *fundamental*, and some errors are *fatal*. This is evident The doctrines which are the foundation-stones, supporting the entire fabric of Christianity, must be believed; for the belief of them is necessary to *form* Christian character, and consequently necessary to salvation: and by the aforesaid rule, "as a man thinketh in his heart," thus receiving or rejecting them, "*so* is he," in the sight of God. It becomes us, therefore, to "search the Scriptures" diligently, that we may be able to discriminate between those doctrines which are necessary and those which are not; "ready always to give an answer to every man that asketh a reason of the hope that is in us." When *immortal* interests are involved, our wisdom is shown in fearlessly encountering whatever may be respectfully said in opposition to our views. To confront statements of principles with sallies of passion, is indeed neither prudent nor safe. We can not afford to decide the validity of our heavenly hopes by such an unseemly contest. The man that has supreme love for truth, will defend his principles by urging facts and proofs, until he convinces or is convinced; and then, in the name of truth, will either demand or yield a surrender. Or if he be debating a point with himself, he will honestly weigh both sides of the question; and because he does so dispassionately, though it may be slowly yet surely shall he arrive at the truth. This is the general issue of all investigation thus made.

Among those doctrines we consider *fundamental,* the Supreme Deity of Christ is preëminent. They who believe that He is God, and they who hold him to be no more than a CREATURE, embrace two doctrines upon which are built up two systems, necessarily as wide apart in their principles, statements, and general results, as the poles of the earth. Theirs is not a simple disagreement, but a total, irreconcilable contradiction, from the beginning to the end. The one is a *positive,* the other a *negative;* what the one *attracts,* the other *repels;* therefore if one be right, the other is wrong; if one be saving truth, the other is ruinous error. The difference may be thus briefly stated. If Christ be not God, but a mere creature, then I am an IDOLATER, and according to the Scriptures, my faith and its results must banish me from heaven. If, on the other hand, Christ be God and not a creature, then they who believe the contrary are involved in this calamity, because "they glorify Him not as God;" and because they "change the glory of the incorruptible God" by degrading him to the level of a creature. If Christ be not God, then is it impossible for me to be saved, for I depend upon his infinite atonement and imputed righteousness for salvation, which no creature can make; but if Christ be God, then they who reject his divinity, in rejecting his atonement and righteousness for their personal justification, because he is but a creature, are consistent with themselves; but by that means they put themselves out of the pale of Gospel hope, "for without the shedding of blood there is no remission."

These things are so, or they are not. If they are so, it would be very unfair to decry this statement on the score of "uncharitableness," because charity itself, which means love to men, naturally urges the investigation here commended. If they are not so, then charity is equally concerned in exposing the fallacy of the subsequent argument. Principles, systems, and their practical results, so far as they relate to the best interests of men, charity demands us to canvass; that truth may be brought out in all its strength, to animate our hopes, to subdue our fears, to invigorate our faith, and to secure our peace. *Charity*, in the cant phrase of the day, means the obsequiousness of an elastic conscience; the ductility of religious principle; by which, out of mere compliment to all men, we should regard their opinions, be they what they may, with equal forbearance and outward respect. This sentiment, however, which the word never did and never can convey, is as false in theory as it is mischievous in practice. According to this, Christ and his apostles were the most uncharitable denouncers that ever lived; and all efforts to recover men from the dangers of error, are the mere outbreakings of an uncharitable spirit!

But we have not so learned the Gospel. "Charity rejoiceth not in iniquity, but rejoiceth in the TRUTH." Because she loves the souls of men, she is faithful in exposing error; and while she holds up the true Gospel, she is bound, at the same time, to rebuke such as "hold the truth in unrighteousness;" and warn men against all that is vitiating to a saving faith, and all that is fatal to a solid hope. If, for instance, the supreme Deity of Christ be a truth, it must be a *fundamental* truth, for out of it grow other truths which the Scriptures teach are necessary to salvation. Therefore we are bound, by every Christian sentiment, to bring this matter to the test of Scripture, pushing opinions to their legitimate consequences, regardless of what cavillers may think or say. From the lovers of truth, sincere, it may be, in an error, there is every thing to hope; from the indifferentist and pseudo-liberal, there is nothing to fear. We know of no other way whereby we may obey the apostolic injunctions: "Earnestly contend for the faith once delivered to the saints." "Prove all things, hold fast that which is good." "Whatsoever things are true, whatsoever things are honest, whatsoever things are just, whatsoever things are pure, whatsoever things are lovely, whatsoever things are of good report, if there be any virtue, and if there be any praise, THINK on these things."

The great question to be settled is this—Do THE SCRIPTURES TEACH THAT JESUS CHRIST IS THE SUPREME GOD? We believe they do most clearly establish this doctrine, and we think it can be shown to the satisfaction of every considerate and candid mind, unshackled by prejudice, and unpledged to a system right or wrong, that this belief necessarily flows from, and consequently is enjoined by the Bible. We, therefore, invite our readers to look at the proof we offer, and which convinces us, on a point we *must* consider vital to Christianity; and we especially invite them that differ from us, *to get rid of the* DILEMMAS, into which, we think, they are placed, without impeaching the Scriptures. Whatever system of faith reduces us to an *absurdity*, must be abandoned. We intend to show that such is the effect of the denial of *the Supreme Godhead of Christ*, and if we succeed in any point out of the many we attempt, in that point we ask for a surrender; not to us, but to TRUTH, for its own sake: if we succeed in but half of our attempt, we ask for the surrender of a faith upon which reliance is thus proved unsafe. We seek nothing but the SALVATION of those who have been misled, as we think; and who are generous enough to renounce ill-formed opinions, whenever they are shown to be so.

CONTENTS.

CHAPTER I.

CHAPTER II.

CHAPTER III.

CHAPTER IV.

CHAPTER V.

CHAPTER VI.

CHAPTER VII.

CHAPTER X.

CONCLUSION.

SUPREME GODHEAD OF CHRIST.

CHAPTER I.

INSPIRATION: Proofs—Extracts from a Unitarian Writer—Consequences of his view—Lowest Inspiration.

As the Bible is our ultimate standard, by which we are to determine all questions of doctrine, we must know to what extent we may rely upon its statements. Is it in whole or in part, "the word of God, and not the word of man"? Are its contents inspired by God, or are they the productions of minds, divinely taught, in the writing of which their authors were kept simply from making mistakes? Is Inspiration plenary or partial? All questions of this sort, must be answered by the Bible itself.

On this subject its statements are not made with hesitancy, but in clear and cogent language. We are told that "God, who at sundry times, and in divers manners, spake in *time past* by the prophets, hath in these *last days* spoken unto us by his Son."*

* Heb. 1 : 1, 2.

We are told that "prophecy came not in old time by the will of man; but holy men of God *spake* as they were *moved* by the Holy Ghost;"* and that these men "prophesied of the grace that should come unto you; searching what, or what manner of time, the *Spirit* of *Christ*, which was in them, did signify, when it testified beforehand the sufferings of Christ."† Our Saviour indorsed the canon of the Old Testament, when he said: "All things must be fulfilled which were written in the law of Moses, and in the Prophets, and in the Psalms, concerning me. Then opened he their understanding, that they might understand the Scriptures."‡ These are the "Holy Scriptures" in which Timothy was educated, and respecting which Paul says: "All Scripture is given by *inspiration* of God, and is profitable for doctrine, for reproof, for correction, for instruction in righteousness."§ Paul says that he "neither received the Gospel of man, neither was *taught* it, but by the *revelation* of Jesus Christ;"‖ and again, speaking in behalf of all the apostles he says: "Which things also *we* speak, not in the *words* which man's wisdom teacheth, but which the Holy Ghost teacheth."¶ And that this inspiration accompanied their pens as well as their tongues, appears from this assurance: "The things that I *write* unto you are the commandments of the Lord."** "By revelation

* 2 Pet. 1 : 21. † 1 Pet. 1 : 11, 12.
‡ Luke 24 : 44, 45. § 2 Tim. 3 : 15, 16. ‖ Gal. 1 : 12.
¶ 1 Cor. 2 : 13. ** 1 Cor. 14 : 37.

he made known unto me the mystery; as I wrote afore in few words; whereby, when ye read, ye may understand my knowledge in the mystery of Christ, which in other ages was not made known unto the sons of men, as it is now *revealed* unto his holy apostles and prophets by the Spirit."*

This direct and unmistakable language teaches us to rely with all confidence upon the facts, statements, assertions, doctrines, etc., of holy Scripture; respecting which there is no misstatement by the writers, no mistake made; the thing was impossible, since the Holy Ghost "taught them all things; and led them into all truth." Because inspired by infallible wisdom, they wrote infallible writings, and gave an infallible rule of faith and practice.

However plain and positive the apostles write on this subject, Unitarians have gone so far as to say: "Indeed, we sometimes find St. Paul committing mistakes, or uttering contradictory counsels, that are far more serious than these slight expressions of uninspired minds." This surprising sentiment is laid down in a work entitled, "How I became a Unitarian, by a Clergyman of the Episcopal Church, 1852." The anonymous author further states, (p. 33):

"I say it was under this solemn and ominous impression," (namely, that the world was to come to an end, and the day of final judgment to appear, before the generation then living should pass away,) "that the Gospels and Epistles were written; and written there-

* Eph. 3: 3–5.

fore, as we may safely affirm, but to meet the demands of a present occasion, without the remotest reference in the minds of the writers to the wants and capacities of a distant era, as ours. And further, neither is it irrelevant nor in any degree hazardous to say, that they would necessarily, therefore, be written in haste; and in a haste that would naturally betray the writers into inaccuracy of statement, in regard to many unimportant facts, as well as give occasion for the expression of individual opinions, which were rather the reflection of the age than the dictate of supernal wisdom. The influence of these facts upon their productions, it would be difficult to estimate. That it was great, we have the evidence before us. So also was it a coöperating influence shown in their zeal, their sufferings, their labors, their patience, their faith, their courage; and above all in their honest simplicity, their truthfulness, their candor. And thus while they win our entire confidence in their veracity, they unconsciously guard us against the error of looking upon them as infallible counsellors, in regard to matters of which we are fully as competent to form a correct judgment as they were!" As an evidence of this, he refers* to "what St. Peter says, when scoffers in his day, observing the language of the preachers of Christianity who predicted the speedy dissolution of the earth, called for the evidence of the approaching catastrophe, and remarked that 'all things continue

* Pp. 36, 37.

as they were from the beginning of the creation.' Upon this the Apostle takes occasion to warn them that the day of the Lord 'cometh as a thief in the night;' and as possibly distrusting his own interpretation of the event, ingeniously qualifies the prediction by saying, that 'a day with the Lord is as a thousand years.'" This is just saying that Peter wrote with duplicity; that he gave forth a sibylline oracle!

Speaking of the way in which we should receive the word of God, he further says, (p. 37:) "Shall we be permitted to make no allowance for human error? for personal failings and prejudices in the writers? for circumscribed views of physical, no less than moral truth? This would be most unreasonable and absurd. Neither is it necessary to a devout and profitable use of the sacred oracles. These errors, however zealously denied, can not be hid. They must be acknowledged and accounted for; and when the keen edge of philosophical criticism is applied to them, they must yield to its painful surgery."

We have made this extended quotation to show, from their own principles, how easy it is for Unitarians to get rid of perplexing texts, which prove the divinity of Christ, and any other doctrine they may see fit to discard. Comparing this *view of inspiration* with the Apostles' declarations, we must see they are irreconcilable. If the New Testament is made up of the truths of the Holy Ghost, interlarded with the errors and mistakes of the individual writers, how are we to know what is the genuine word of God, and what is not? Does not this view pave the way for the last bold steps of *Deism?* What security have we that any of the Scriptures are genuine, or that the apostles and prophets were inspired at all? Besure, they say so; but then, they may have been *mistaken*, and thus be false guides. Admit the principle of this quotation, and our rule of faith is a rope of sand, unworthy of the high claims set up for it by the writers of the same. If Peter might "distrust his own interpretation" in one case, so may we distrust him in others, and thus it is easy to escape the force of any proof derived from the Bible, for any doctrine of Christianity.

It is a significant fact, that necessity is thus felt for depreciating the word of God. The doctrine for which we contend, can not be reached without this preliminary work. Degrade the word of God, then it is easy to degrade the Son of God. Let it be subjected to the "keen edge of philosophical criticism," such as is in favor with Unitarians, and it may be made subservient to all the purposes of erroneous speculation that the most discordant religionists can entertain. This involves an absurdity whose vastness makes it harmless in the view of every right-minded man. If the Scriptures are a *revelation* from God to us, teaching us what we must believe and do, in order to salvation, to answer the purpose, they must have been secured from all the perversions of prejudice, and from all admixture of error;

otherwise, they could not be a revelation at all. We, therefore, shall assume that in regard to fact and doctrine, and the various statements they contain, they are "the truth, the whole truth, and nothing but the truth."

The lowest kind of inspiration, that can be well thought of, is that called the "*Inspiration of Superintendence*," which means the care God took of the writers, that what they stated should be free from the possibility of error. The Scriptures must have been inspired at *least* in this sense, or they were inspired not at all. We think there can be no debate here among reasonable men, and upon this ground we hope to show, that the deniers of our Lord's divinity are entangled in dilemmas, out of which they can not get.

CHAPTER II.

I. Dilemma: *Either Christ is the Supreme God, or there is no name by which God can be distinguished from His creatures.*
Collation of Scripture—Qualifications of Paul—Proofs from New Testament—Consequences—Verification of Dilemma.

We proceed now to prove, that every name, single or complicate, by which we recognize the Supreme God as distinctly pointed out in the Scriptures of the Old Testament, beyond dispute is applied by inspiration to the Lord Jesus Christ in the Scriptures of the New Testament by way of commentary and explication.

The *first* class of passages we present, embraces Old-Testament texts quoted and referred to by New-Testament writers. We substitute the word "Jehovah" for "Lord," because it is acknowledged to be the true rendering wherever the latter is printed in small capitals, and is the *incommunicable* name of the Supreme Being.

(1.) Ps. 16 : 8.—I have set Jehovah always before me; because he is always at my right hand, I shall not be moved.

Acts 2 : 25.—For David speaketh concerning him, (Christ,) I foresaw the Lord always before my face; he is on my right hand, that I should not be moved.

It is quite clear from the discourse of Peter in this chapter, that he argumentatively applies his quotation from David directly to CHRIST, as the one *meant;* but David speaks of Jehovah; therefore CHRIST is JEHOVAH, or Peter was utterly mistaken, and although inspired, imposed upon his hearers a false argument, designing to mislead them, if not mislead himself.

(2.) Is. 40 : 3.—The voice of him that crieth in the wilderness, Prepare ye the way of JEHOVAH, make straight in the desert a highway for OUR GOD.

Mat. 3 : 3.—For this is He that was spoken of by the prophet Esaias, saying, The voice of one crying in the wilderness, prepare ye the way of the LORD, make his paths straight.

The Evangelist says, argumentatively, that John the Baptist was the person *meant* by the prophet; but John's voice was heard in the wilderness, in preparation of the way for CHRIST; therefore CHRIST is JEHOVAH, or Matthew deceives us, either through ignorance or by design.

(3.) Is. 6 : 3–5.—And one cried unto another, and said, Holy, holy, holy is JEHOVAH OF HOSTS; the whole earth is full of HIS GLORY. . . . . . mine eyes have seen the KING, JEHOVAH OF HOSTS.

John 12 : 41.—These things said Esaias when he SAW HIS GLORY, AND SPAKE OF HIM.

This is peculiarly strong. We ask the reader to peruse the context of each passage. It will be seen that the prophet is favored with a magnificent vision, and dreads the consequence of having seen the King, Jehovah of Hosts. At the same time he is sent to the people with this message: "Hear ye indeed, but understand not; and see ye indeed, but perceive not. Make the heart of this people fat, and make their ears heavy, and shut their eyes; lest they see with their eyes, and hear with their ears, and understand with their hearts, and convert and be healed."

Now John, in describing the labors of CHRIST, said that the people did not believe, and accounted for it by quoting, *argumentatively*, the aforesaid message; and declared that what the prophet in vision then saw, was the glory of CHRIST, and that he spoke of HIM when he said: "Mine eyes have seen the King, Jehovah of Hosts." The inference is unavoidable, either John, by inspiration, deceives his readers, or CHRIST is the KING, JEHOVAH of HOSTS. There is no escape.

(4.) Ex. 17 : 2.—And Moses said unto them, Wherefore do ye *tempt* JEHOVAH.

Ps. 28 : 56.—They *tempted* and provoked the MOST HIGH GOD.

1 Cor. 10 : 9.—Neither let us *tempt* CHRIST, as some of them also tempted, and were destroyed of serpents.

There is no doubt that Moses, David, and Paul referred to the same historical *fact*.

According to Moses, the Israelites tempted *Jehovah;* and according to David, they tempted the *most high God*. But Paul says they tempted *Christ;* therefore Christ is both Jehovah and the Most High God, otherwise Paul deceives us.

(5.) Ps. 68 : 17, 18.—The chariots of God are twenty thousand, even thousands of angels. JEHOVAH is among them as in Sinai, in the holy place. Thou hast ascended on high, *thou hast led captivity captive: thou hast received gifts for men.*

Eph. 4 : 7, 8.—But unto every one of us is grace given according to the measure of the gift of CHRIST. Wherefore he saith, when HE ascended up on high, *he led captivity captive, and gave gifts unto men.*

In the first of these quotations, the Psalmist addresses Jehovah as the one who ascended on high, leading captivity captive. In the second, Paul argumentatively applies these words to Christ as the one whom David *meant.* Therefore Christ is Jehovah, or Paul deceives again.

(6.) Is. 8 : 13, 14.—Sanctify JEHOVAH OF HOSTS HIMSELF, and let HIM be your fear, and let HIM be your dread. And HE shall be for a sanctuary: but for a STONE OF STUMBLING AND A ROCK OF OFFENSE, to both houses of Israel.

1 Pet. 2 : 7, 8.—Unto you therefore which believe, he (Christ) is precious: but unto them which be disobedient, the stone which the builders disallowed, the same is made the head of the corner, and A STONE OF STUMBLING, AND A ROCK OF OFFENSE, to them which stumble at the word, being disobedient.

According to the Prophet, Jehovah of Hosts himself is a stone of stumbling, and a rock of offense, but according to the Apostle, CHRIST is this stone and rock. Therefore he is Jehovah of Hosts himself: otherwise Peter deceives us.

(7.) Is. 43 : 3.—For I am JEHOVAH THY GOD, THE HOLY ONE OF ISRAEL, THY SAVIOUR.

2 Pet. 3 : 18.—OUR LORD AND SAVIOUR JESUS CHRIST.

We must remember that the epithets descriptive of Christ in the New Testament are *borrowed* from the

Old. He who is our Saviour, according to the prophet, is Jehovah God, the Holy One; but he who is our Saviour, according to the Apostle, is Jesus Christ. Therefore Christ is Jehovah God, and the Holy One; or Peter deceives worse than he did, when he said, "I know not the man!"

(8.) Zech. 12 : 10.—And I (Jehovah) will pour upon the house of David, and upon the inhabitants of Jerusalem, the spirit of grace and of supplication: and they shall look upon ME whom they have PIERCED, and they shall mourn.

John 19 : 38.—And again another Scripture saith, They shall look on HIM (*Christ*) whom they PIERCED.

According to the Prophet, the one who is pierced is Jehovah; but according to the Apostle's inspired *explanation*, Christ is the one *meant;* for to him he applies this prophecy. Therefore *Christ* is JEHOVAH, or John either ignorantly or deceitfully perverts the prophecy!

(9.) Micah 5 : 2.—But thou, Bethlehem Ephratah, though thou be little among the thousands of Judah, yet out of thee shall come forth unto me that is to be RULER in Israel: whose goings forth have been from of old, from EVERLASTING.

Mat. 2 : 6.—And thou Bethlehem, in the land of Juda, art not least among the princes of Juda: for out of thee shall come a governor that shall RULE my people Israel.

According to the Prophet, this Ruler has been from *eternity*, and the eternity of the *past* can never be predicated of a *created* being: therefore he must mean the uncreated God. But the Evangelist says this prophecy was pointed out by the Jews as to be fulfilled in *Christ*, who, consequently, must have existed from the eternity of the past, and is therefore the EVERLASTING RULER. Matthew evidently approves the reference.

(10.) Is. 43 : 11.—I, even I, am JEHOVAH : and besides me there is NO SAVIOUR.

Acts 4 : 12.—For there is none other NAME under heaven given among men whereby we must be SAVED.

The Prophet declares there is no Saviour but HE whose name is JEHOVAH, and the Apostle declares there is no Saviour but HE whose name is CHRIST. Therefore Christ is Jehovah, or else an inspired evangelist irreconcilably contradicts an inspired prophet.

(11.) Jer. 23 : 24.—Do not I FILL heaven and earth, saith JEHOVAH.

Eph. 1 : 23.—The fullness of him (CHRIST) that FILLETH all in all.

The Prophet declares Jehovah fills heaven and earth, which means universal space. The Apostle affirms that Christ fills all in all, which must mean the same thing. Therefore Christ is the Omnipresent Jehovah, or else Paul asserts what can not be true!

(12.) Ps. 89 : 8, 9.—O JEHOVAH GOD OF HOSTS, who is a STRONG JEHOVAH like unto thee? or to thy faithfulness round about thee? Thou rulest the raging of the sea : when the waves thereof arise, THOU stillest them.

Mark 4 : 39 : 40.—And HE arose, and rebuked the wind, and said unto the sea, *Peace, be still.* And there was a great calm. And they feared exceedingly, and said one to another, what manner of *man* is this, that even the winds and the sea obey him?

That Jehovah God of Hosts is the strong Jehovah, like unto whom there is no other, David argues from the fact of its being *his* prerogative to quell the commotion of the sea. But Christ in his own name did precisely the *same* thing: and the exclamation of his disciples, "What *manner of man* is this!" showed that independent exercise of divine power, in the way of which David speaks, was to them the first proof of the Godhead of Christ, a doctrine they more fully understood afterwards, and most clearly unfolded. Now, if the Psalmist reasoned rightly, then *Christ* must be the STRONG JEHOVAH; but if he be only a *creature*, then his argument is good for nothing, and he was himself deceived.

(13.) Prov. 16 : 4.—JEHOVAH made all things FOR HIMSELF.

Col. 1 : 16.—All things were created BY HIM, and FOR HIM, that is, for Christ.

Therefore Christ is Jehovah, or Paul has misstated the great end of creation.

(14.) Is. 9 : 6.—FOR UNTO US A CHILD IS BORN, unto us a son is given, and the government shall be upon his shoulder; and his *name* shall be called WONDERFUL, COUNSELLOR, THE MIGHTY GOD, THE EVERLASTING FATHER, THE PRINCE OF PEACE.

Luke 2 : 11.—For UNTO YOU IS BORN THIS DAY, in the city of David, a Saviour, which is Christ the Lord.

Rev. 19 : 12.—And he (Christ) had a *name* written that *no man knew* but he himself.

Rev. 3 : 18.—I (Jesus) COUNSEL thee, etc.

Rev. 1 : 8.—I (Jesus) am—the ALMIGHTY.

John 8 : 58.—Before Abraham was I AM.

Acts. 3 : 15.—The PRINCE of life.

Here it will be seen, that the several descriptions given of the *child born*, by the Prophet, are given of the *child born* of Mary, by the Apostles.

(15.) Ps. 45 : 6.—Thy throne, O God, is for ever and ever, the sceptre of thy kingdom is a right sceptre.

Heb. 1 : 8.—But unto the SON he saith, Thy throne, O God, is for ever and ever, a sceptre of righteousness is the sceptre of thy kingdom.

In the first of these passages David addresses nono but the Great God; for whose throne besides his, is for ever and ever? But Paul declares that he addresses *Christ.* Therefore Christ is God, whose throne endures for ever; or the argument is deceptive by design of inspiration! The Apostle quotes the Psalmist beyond all doubt, *word for word*, as it is in the Hebrew. To get rid of this overwhelming passage, Unitarians resort to the miserable expedient of altering the words of Paul to make him say: "God is thy throne"! To support their denial of the divinity of Christ, they find it necessary to practise unfairly with Paul, by making him misquote a passage he adduces in argument! One of their writers, however, says: "It is possible, and even probable, in reference to Hebrews 1 : 8, 'Thy throne, O *God!* is for ever and ever,' that the writer of an epistle addressed to Hebrews, abounding as it does in Jewish phraseology, should have spoken of Christ as *a* God, or mighty prince, whose throne of righteousness was to be perpetual and immovable, in imitation of his illustrious forefathers, who, as instanced, both in the Psalms, from which the passage is quoted, and in other places of the Old Testament, were wont to use the appellation *God* in a lower sense, with far greater frequency than the writers of the New Testament." ! !* Such a defense we claim as a virtual *surrender*. Its implication is monstrous.

(17.) Ps. 102 : 24-27.—I said, O my God, take me not away in the midst of my days: thy years are throughout all genera-

* SCRIPTURE PROOFS OF UNITARIANISM.—A foreign work, republished by The Unitarian Association of the State of New York, whose author is a Humanitarian, that is, one who believes that Christ was nothing more than a *mere man*.

In their preface to that performance, they have this *caveat:* "We think it proper to remark that, the author's Humanitarianism would be objected to by many Unitarians in this country, and we do not intend, therefore, to indorse his sentiments respecting the nature of Christ, any further than they *deny or disprove his supreme Deity*." We respectfully suggest, that the Association might enlarge the number of its rare publications by the addition of several works forcibly written by respectable *Deists*, who are cordial towards the upholders of Unitarian sentiments. If judged important, a *caveat* similar to the above, might be put in a preface. A tract or two from the Koran of Mohammed, with suitable observations, might not be amiss. Any thing to disprove the Supreme Deity of Christ! Any thing to help in the great labor to *prove a negative!*

But why this *caveat?* What is "the nature of Christ"? Had he preëxistence? If so, then either he existed in a "nature" superior, or equal, or inferior to that of angels. If *superior*, then in his union with the rational soul and organized body of Jesus, we have the Unitarian objection, that there were *two* persons in the *same* individual. If his "nature" was *equal*, then he was an angel, and therefore the same difficulty occurs; Christ was not *man* at all, but had only the outer shell of humanity. If he was *inferior*, then Paul was greatly mistaken; then his human soul preëxisted, and if all souls do not preëxist in the same way, he had not the nature of *man;* if they do, then the doctrine of *metempsychosis* is true.

tions. Of old hast THOU laid the foundations of the earth: and the heavens are the work of THY hands. They shall perish, but thou shalt endure: yea, all of them shall wax old like a garment; as a vesture shalt thou change them, and they shall be changed. But thou art the same, and thy years shall have no end.

Heb. 1 : 10, 11, 12.—But unto the SON he saith——And THOU, LORD, in the beginning hast laid the foundation of the earth; and the heavens are the works of THY hands. They shall perish, but thou remainest: and they shall wax old as doth a garment; and as a vesture shalt thou fold them up, and they shall be changed: but thou art the same, and thy years shall not fail.

David here addressed the self-existent God, who is the First Cause of all things, and who shall change all things; but Paul, for the *purpose of argument*, says David used these words as descriptive of the nature and works of Christ. Therefore, Christ is the self-existent God; otherwise, Paul is guilty of blasphemy.

(18.) Ps. 31 : 5.—Into thy hands I commit my spirit; thou hast redeemed me, O JEHOVAH, GOD OF TRUTH.

Acts 7 : 59—And they stoned Stephen, calling upon, and saying, LORD JESUS receive my spirit.

This devout prayer of David, the martyr adopts in his last moments, addressing our Saviour. Therefore, the Lord Jesus is Jehovah God of truth; or Stephen was guilty of blasphemy, and rightly put to death, according to the law of God, by stoning. He deceived himself and deceived others, in the last act of his life!

(19.) Gen. 17 : 1.—And when Abram was ninety years old and nine, JEHOVAH appeared to Abram and said unto him, I am the ALMIGHTY God.

Rev. 1 : 8.—I (Christ) am Alpha and Omega, the beginning and the ending, saith the Lord, which is, and which was, and which is to come, the ALMIGHTY.

In the first of these quotations, Jehovah announces his name to Abram as the Almighty. In the second, the Alpha and the Omega, announces the the same thing; therefore He is the *Almighty*. To determine who the *speaker* is, in this verse—whether it be the Father or the Son, we ask attention to the following observations.

(1.) The first verse opens with announcing the *object* of the book—namely "The *Apocalypse* of Jesus Christ." The meaning of this is to be determined by parallel passages. 1 Cor. 1 : 7, "Waiting for the *apocalypse* or *revealing*, (rendered in our version coming) of our Lord Jesus Christ." 2 Thess. 1 : 7, "And to you who are troubled, rest with us, at the *apocalypse* (coming) of our Lord Jesus Christ." 1 Pet. 1 : 7. At the *apocalypse* (coming) of Jesus Christ, v. 13—"The grace that is to be brought unto you at the *apocalypse* (coming) of Jesus Christ." 1 Peter 4 : 13, "When his glory shall be *apocalypsed*" (revealed) namely, at his coming. This book, then, is no *revelation* of things made *to* Christ; but it is the manifestation of the *coming of Christ*, which Deity, as such, gave to the triumphant Messiah, as such, to communicate to his servants by the hand of John. The Revelation differs from the first performance of John, that is, his Gospel, which was the manifestation of the Messiah who had come in his humiliation; this being a manifestation of the Messiah yet to come in his exaltation, and as such, in his official capacity, he is of course distinguished from the Deity.

(2.) Beyond a doubt, Christ is meant in v. 7, "Behold he cometh——yea, truly (elliptically connecting with v. 8) I am Alpha and Omega, the BEGINNING and the ENDING, saith the Lord, which is, and which was, and which is to come, the Almighty." This is the great announcement. John now stops, to supply the ellipsis between vs. 7 and 8, by relating the circumstances under which this announcement was made; and having said it proceeded from "a great voice," he goes on in v. 11 to *repeat* the first words uttered—"I am Alpha and Omega, the FIRST and the LAST." We have to determine one thing more. Whose voice was this? 12th v. "And I turned to see the voice that spake with me, and being turned I saw——one like unto the Son of God—(vs. 17 and 18.) And when I saw him, I fell at his feet as dead, and he laid his right hand upon me, saying, Fear not; I am the FIRST and the LAST; he that liveth, and was dead." Therefore CHRIST is the speaker in v. 8.

(3.) This is placed beyond reasonable dispute by Rev. 22 : 12, 13, "And behold I come quickly—I am Alpha and Omega, the BEGINNING and the ENDING, the FIRST and the LAST." Mark the grouping of the epithets in Chap. 1, vs. 8 and 11. Now who is the "*I*" here? See Rev. 22 : 16. "*I Jesus.*"

(4.) But Unitarians say, the amended text of v. 8th reads thus—SAITH THE LORD GOD—which is never applied to Christ. Let us see. We accept the amendment, and refer to Rev. 22 : 6: " And THE LORD GOD of the holy prophets, sent HIS angel to show unto his servant the things which must shortly be done." Who is he? v. 16: "I JESUS have sent MINE *angel* to testify unto you these things." Can any thing be plainer?

(5.) It is further said, the phrase, "Who is, and who was, and who is to come," is a Jewish formula, significant of the eternal God, and is never applied to Christ. Admitting this for a moment, we present another Jewish formula, significant of the *same* thing, about which there can be no mistake. Heb. 13 : 8, "Jesus Christ, the *same yesterday, and to-day and for ever.*" The one formula expresses *eternity* as much and as intensely as the other.

(20.) 1 Ch. 28 : 6.—JEHOVAH *searcheth* all hearts, and understandeth all the imaginations of the thoughts.

Rev. 2 : 23.—I am HE which *searcheth* the reins and hearts.

According to David, Jehovah searcheth the heart, and this is his prerogative *alone.* 1 Kings 8 : 39. But according to John, JESUS exercises the same prerogative. Therefore He is Jehovah, or John deceives us.

(21.) Prov. 3 : 12.—For whom JEHOVAH loveth, he correcteth.

Rev. 3 : 19.—As many as I love, I rebuke and chasten.

CHRIST adopts these words as applicable to himself, which are descriptive of the mercy and dealings of Jehovah with his children. Therefore HE is Jehovah.

(22.) Is. 40 : 10.—Behold the LORD GOD will come with strong hand, and his arms shall rule for him: behold *his reward* is with HIM and HIS work before him.

Rev. 22 : 12.—Behold I (Jesus) come quickly; and *my reward* is with ME to give every man according as his work shall be.

What the Prophet declares of the Lord God who will come, Christ declares of himself as about to come quickly. Therefore HE is the LORD GOD, or else he uses the language of the Bible deceitfully!

(23.) Is. 44 : 6.—Thus saith JEHOVAH, THE KING OF ISRAEL and his Redeemer, JEHOVAH OF HOSTS, I AM THE FIRST AND THE LAST: AND BESIDES ME THERE IS NO GOD.

Rev. 22 : 13.—I (Jesus) am Alpha and Omega, the beginning and the end, THE FIRST AND THE LAST.

According to the Prophet, he who is the *first and the last*, is Jehovah of Hosts, besides whom there is no God. But according to the Apostle, Christ is the *first and the last;* therefore *He* is Jehovah of Hosts, besides whom there is no God. If this be not so, then the Saviour of the world inspired John to deceive the world!!

(24.) Deut. 10 : 17.—JEHOVAH your God, is God of gods, and LORD of LORDS.

Jer. 10 : 10.—But JEHOVAH is an EVERLASTING KING.

1 Tim. 6 : 15, 16.—The blessed and only Potentate, THE KING OF KINGS AND LORD OF LORDS; who only hath immortality, dwelling in the light which no man can approach unto; whom no man hath seen, nor can see; to whom be honor and power everlasting. Amen.

Rev. 17 : 14.—The Lamb shall overcome them; for HE IS KING OF KINGS AND LORD OF LORDS

Rev. 19 : 16.—He hath on his vesture, and on his thigh a name written, KING OF KINGS AND LORD OF LORDS.

These texts speak for themselves. They show that the high and glorious title of Jehovah, embodied in one of the most magnificent descriptions of Deity to be found in the Bible, is not only said to belong to Christ, but to be *written* upon him, describing what he is and ever shall be. He to whom the doxology is rendered, (1 Tim. 1 : 17,) "Now unto the King, eternal, immortal, invisible, the only wise God, be honor and glory for ever," is "the King of kings and Lord of lords;" but this glorious divine title belongs to CHRIST, who showed himself unto John in Patmos, in awful majesty, having this title written upon his thigh. How is it possible to escape the conclusion that Christ is God? If he is not, how is it possible to escape the conviction that John has deceived us; and if he spoke by the Spirit, was inspired by God himself to deceive his creatures!

(25.) Jer. 10 : 10.—JEHOVAH IS THE TRUE GOD, HE IS THE LIVING GOD.

1 John 5 : 20.—We are in him that is true, even in his Son, Jesus Christ. THIS IS THE TRUE GOD AND ETERNAL LIFE.

Comment is unnecessary, but an anecdote is in point.

"Two gentlemen were once disputing on the divinity of Christ. One of them who argued against it said: 'If it were true, it certainly would have been expressed in more clear and unequivocal terms.' 'Well,' said the other, 'admitting that you believed it, were you authorized to teach it, and allowed to use your own language, how would you express the doctrine to make it indubitable?' 'I would say,' replied he, 'that Jesus Christ is *the true* God.' 'You are very happy,' rejoined the other, 'in the choice of your words; for you have happened to hit upon the words of inspiration. St. John, speaking of the Son, says, "This is the true God and eternal life.'"*

We now give from the apostolic writings, a second class of passages, which were evidently meant to be didactic; and consequently, formative of Christian faith. Paul declared, that God had "called him by his grace, to *reveal* his Son in him that he might preach Him among the heathen." We must therefore conclude that he had very definite ideas of the nature of Christ, and was well able so to speak, that his language should be free from ambiguity; and should convey nothing, even by implication, that might lead to gross mistake. We must believe, that with the twofold advantage of *inspiration* and *education*, he would be able so to instruct the heathen, that they should clearly apprehend his meaning; that he would be particularly careful, on vital points, that they should have no excuse in his phraseology for misunderstanding him; and especially in his statement of facts, that they should know exactly what he meant. God chose him for this purpose, and he was faithful in the

* Anecdotes on Catechism.

discharge of his duty. Let us therefore see what he has to say about his exalted Lord.

(1.) Rom. 9 : 5.—Whose are the fathers, and of whom, *as concerning the flesh*, Christ came, who is *over all*, GOD BLESSED FOR EVER.

This text certainly is very clear. The heathen could understand it. They would know, that Christ was a Jew; but if he were no more than a man, they would have had some little merriment over the solemn assurance that a *man* came, "as concerning the flesh;" or if he were the highest of the various orders of God's creatures, they would have had great trouble with the implication so intensely absurd, that one creature united to another creature is the Creator! But the antithetical form of this verse, so plainly teaches that he was man *according to the flesh*, and something else *not according to the flesh;* which something else, is defined to be, "who is over all, God blessed for ever," they could not have had any doubt as to the intention and language of Paul. The plain statement of what Christ is, as to his *human nature*, in the first part of the text, implies that the statement in the last part declares what he is, *otherwise than according to the flesh:* that is, it is a plain statement of his *divine* nature, God blessed for ever.

Manuscripts, versions, and various readings do not help Unitarians here. They are obliged to acknowledge the integrity of the received original, and are forced to the admission, that as the common translation does no violence either to grammar or idiom, it *may* be the true one. But in order to show that this is not a *decisive* passage, they tell us it *may* be differently pointed. Thus by altering the punctuation, and by thrusting the word "God" out of its natural place, and between the relative and its proper antecedent, and by changing the participle into a passive verb, they present this version: "Of whom, concerning the flesh, Christ came. God, who is over all, be blessed for ever." By this *begging of the question*, they hope to invalidate this powerful proof-text. But it is all in vain. Their interpretation is inconsistent with the construction of the original, and decides nothing but their ingenuity at torture, by which the enemies of Christ's divinity endeavor to pervert the Scriptures. This text, moreover, is strongly confirmed by Rom. 1 : 3, 4, where Christ is shown to be Son of man *according to the flesh*, that is, human nature; and the Son of God *according to the Spirit of Holiness*, that is, divine nature. The antithesis in both cases is equally strong. (See Acts 2 : 30.) Now, if Christ is only a man, how comes it that no other distinguished man mentioned in the Scriptures is represented as coming, *according to the flesh?* If he is more than man, according to this text, he must be the Supreme God; but if he is only man, Paul wrote unintelligibly, and was not fit to preach the Gospel to the heathen. Both his learning and his inspiration did not keep him from penning a good grammatical and idiomatic sentence, whose obvious sense taught them simply to change their form of IDOLATRY, by dropping their old idols, and taking a new and a worse one in their stead!

Miserable indeed, must be that system that can thus abuse the word of God, rather than yield to its plain statement of a vital truth.

(2.) 1 Cor. 2 : 7, 8.—But we speak the wisdom of God in a mystery, even the hidden wisdom, which God ordained before the world unto our glory: which none of the princes of this world knew: for had they known it, they would not have crucified the *Lord of Glory*.

This is a Hebraism for Glorious Lord—a title applied to the Deity in the Old Testament. (Is. 33 : 21. Ps. 24 : 8, 10. See also Acts 7 : 2.) Thus it appears Paul borrowed a phrase used in the Old Testament to *describe* the Supreme God, and thereby *described* Christ. If he were an honest man, then we must thus argue: He who was crucified as to his manhood, is the Lord of Glory, that is, JEHOVAH, or the passage is unmeaning. If Unitarianism be true, Paul's character suffers.

(3.) Phil. 2 : 6, 8.—Christ, who being in the form of God, thought it not robbery to be equal with God: but made himself of no reputation, and took upon him the form of a servant, and was made in the likeness of men, and being found in fashion as a man, he humbled himself, and became obedient unto death, even the death of the cross.

This passage proves one of two things, either Christ is God, or the *very worst man that ever existed!* Let us examine it.

(1.) Christ is God. He is said to have subsisted

in the "form of God." But as God has no outward form, this expression must refer to his *nature*, and must be interpreted by the parallel phrase "the form of a servant." Now, was our Saviour a real servant? Certainly, He says himself: "I am among you as one that serveth." He did the work of a servant in washing his disciples' feet when girded with a towel. He is expressly called a servant by prophecy: "Behold my *servant* whom I uphold." When our Lord therefore took the *form* of a servant, he became a *real* servant. Therefore his being in the *form* of God, must mean he was *really* God. This is put beyond dispute by the very next sentence. If he thought it not robbery to be *equal* with God, then he was *God*. And if he was made "in the likeness of men," then he was *man*. Surely, here is the most explicit declaration of the two-fold nature of Christ, He was God and man in one person; language can not be plainer. But the Apostle elsewhere explains it. "Ye know the grace of our Lord Jesus Christ, that though HE WAS rich, yet for your sakes HE BECAME poor, that ye through his poverty, might be rich." Now, we think it quite pertinent to ask—when, where, and how was Christ rich? If his riches were intellectual power, moral greatness, etc., as Unitarians assert, then we ask, when did he become poor? Did he ever cease to be rich in these respects? No. But the contrast must be preserved, and if these were the riches referred to, he must at some time have been divested of his virtue, and shorn of his power, when he became poor. If his poverty, however, referred to his lowly state in the *form of a servant*, then his riches referred to his exalted nature in the *form of God.*

(2.) If he was not God, but a man or some other creature, this passage makes him out the very worst creature; for what greater act of *horrid impiety and blasphemy* is there than this, that a finite creature should arrogate to himself an *equality* with the infinite Creator? Besides, this passage thus interpreted, makes out, not only that he was not God, but that he was not man; for if he only bore a *resemblance* to God, he only bore a resemblance to a servant, he was not a man, but only the *likeness* of a man! Again, this interpretation destroys the whole force of the passage. The Apostle is urging the practice of humility and condescension by the example of Christ. But if he was only a creature, he was bound to obey the will of his Creator, and it was neither humility nor condescension in him to do his duty. If he had disobeyed, he would have been a rebel—as much so as a fallen angel. Where, then, is the exalted honor for which he is lauded by raptured prophets and apostles? Duty, although commendable, is not meritorious. And after all that he had done, he could claim no reward, more than Gabriel or Paul. Thus it is evident that Christ must be God, or the worst specimen of arrogance and pride the universe can exhibit. He must be God, or he was not man. He must be God, or he exhibited neither humility nor condescension. He must be God, or the Apostle's inspired argument is pointless, weak, and worthless!

Unitarians have another way of disposing of this text, which we take to be an implication of their inability to manage it. It is this: "Jesus being, before his incarnation, existent in a godlike form, thought it not therefore robbery to aspire to a god-like preëminence above other celestial creatures, by the work of redemption he now contemplated since the creation and fall of man; and which he foresaw God would so reward."* We need only say, that this is any thing but explaining the words of the Apostle; it is, in fact, an admission that they can not be made to harmonize with Unitarian faith.

There is another important consideration offered, to take off the edge from this and similar texts which Paul wrote. We quote the author just referred to, (pp. 56, 57, 58:) "That Paul was a man of warm temperament, lively imagination, and great activity of mind and body, is quite apparent in what he has written, as well as in what is said of him in the book of the Acts of the Apostles. His zeal, his eloquence, his learning, his courage, his faith, his deep, fervent piety—all these mark him for a man as great as he was good. But he had his faults, notwithstanding; and he is not ashamed to confess them. He was not always equal. He was sometimes overborne by a consciousness of his own feebleness, of the unprepossessing style of his appearance,

* "How I became a Unitarian," p. 73.

by his stammering speech—and he appeared before his audiences 'in fear and much trembling.' He was also at times exceedingly timid. He took Timothy and circumcised him contrary to his own convictions, 'for fear of the Jews.' He was superstitious; he shaved his head, and went up to the temple, after he had said repeatedly and expressly, that 'Christ was the end of the law for righteousness to every one that believed,' and that the temple services were not only obsolete, but nugatory, and therefore virtually forbidden the Christian. He preached baptism for the dead." "He was, likewise, as we should naturally expect, in a man of his enthusiasm, given occasionally to exaggeration. Take, as an instance, his declaration that he could wish himself 'accursed from Christ,' for his brethren and kinsmen according to the flesh. A most extraordinary expression, were it even confined to a person making no claims to inspiration. *Extravagant* is the term we should apply to it, whatever might be the state of excited feeling under which it was spoken. Least of all would we refer it to the dictation of the Holy Spirit."

"Regarded as a man of this character, was St. Paul a person likely to remain unaffected by the current opinions and belief of his day? It seems to me that he was not."—"The very atmosphere in which he moved had been peopled with imaginary deities; the rivers, the woods, the grottos, the fountains, the hills, all had their divinities; and the constellations in the heavens were parcelled out among those superior beings who controlled the destinies of men and nations. St. Paul was not only aware of these facts, but they had formed part of that mental nutriment by which his mind grew to maturity. And now, in his manhood, though converted to Christianity, though no longer *reverencing* idle superstitions, he might not have been an entire unbeliever in the existence of those fabulous deities." To prove this point, this writer refers us to 1 Cor. 8 : 5, 6, and remarks: "What I say in relation to this passage is simply this—that it does not impeach the soundness of Paul's Christianity; it only militates against the idea of his being *infallibly inspired.*" "But I can not say as much for him, when I find him in Col. 2 : 18, inculcating the worshipping of angels"! (P. 62.) "And so St. Paul himself made a God of Jesus in subordination to the Father; and Christians in our day would have us worship him." (P. 64.) "As to what he says, Heb. 1 : 6, about *God* commanding the angels to worship him, all I desire to say is, that it is one of those unfortunate quotations which labor under that first of all necessities, the want of an author. We have no reason to suppose that God ever said any such thing. God never commanded the worshipping of a creature. St. Paul may have thought so, because he adopted the practice"!

We are here informed that Paul was a very good man, but withal, was ardent, impetuous, irresolute, inconsistent, superstitious, naturally prone to stretch the truth, and, notwithstanding his Christianity, a little given to idolatry. Hence he made Christ a God, and in order to sustain his position, made a quotation which really had no author! We remind our readers of a former remark, that Unitarians find themselves necessitated to degrade the word of God, before they can degrade the Son of God. Here we find one, who was once an Episcopal clergyman, anonymously degrading the character of the great Apostle, in order to disparage his writings, and bring them into disrepute, simply because he can no otherwise dispose of his clearly-stated doctrine of the divinity of Christ. We say this is a very significant fact. An avowed Deist could not have done more; certainly, an honest one would not have done as much. Behold the work of Unitarianism! "The tree is known by its fruit."

(4.) Col. 2 : 9.—For in Him (Christ) dwelleth all the fullness of the Godhead bodily.

This phraseology is as strong as strength can make it. If it does not declare the supreme Godhead of Christ, it is the announcement of a solemn *nothing*. It is vexatiously unintelligible, and mischievously worded. *Godhead* means the nature of God. *Fullness* means the contents of a measure, or that with which it is filled up to the brim. "The fullness of the Godhead," then, must mean all that which the Divine Nature contains; as, self-existence, eternity, immensity, independence, immutability, omniscience, omnipresence, omnipotence, and every other attribute essential to Godhead. To go the whole length of the capability of language, the Apostle adds, "*All* the fullness of Deity," or the total sum of what God is. This he affirms, *dwelleth* in Christ, using the present tense, to show that this fullness is not transient, but ever abides in him. Moreover, it dwells in him *bodily*, that is, really, not figuratively; as body means substance, or essence, so bodily means substantially, or essentially. And because the fullness of the Godhead is said to *dwell*, that necessarily supposes a habitation for *indwelling;* consequently the pronoun HIM, must mean Christ's human nature, in which the whole of Deity permanently resides.

Nothing else can be made out of this text without the grossest violation of language. It is much stronger than any simple affirmation of Christ's Deity could be, for Paul purposely chose his language to suit his two principal classes of opponents, namely, the Jews and the Gnostics, a sect of philosophers who incorporated heathen notions with the Gospel. The Jews believed that in the Shekina, or visible cloud in the Temple over the mercy-seat, the Godhead really and substantially dwelt; hence Paul uses the term *bodily*, to convey to the mind of the Jew, the idea that God just as really and substantially dwelt in the *man* Christ Jesus. The Gnostics, on the other hand, made a distinction between the *essence* and the *attributes* of Godhead. They considered the Infinite One, as to his Being, to be withdrawn into the profoundest depth of concealment; and hence they called him the *Abyss:* but the emanations of his essence, that is, his *attributes*, they personified, each of which they supposed to have a separate but subordinate divine existence. When they spoke of the Eternal Being and his attributes, all taken together as one whole, they used the word FULLNESS, meaning thereby every thing that could be comprehended in Godhead. Now it is evident, that the Apostle uses this same word designedly, so as to avoid all mistake on their part. He meant to affirm what ought never to have been misunderstood, namely, that what they considered the FULLNESS OF GOD, dwelleth in Christ.

It is clear, then, that the descriptive phraseology of this text, is much more forcible than the bare assertion that Christ is God; for the Jews sometimes called their magistrates gods, though not so as to make this term ambiguous in its reference, and the Gnostics called the personified attributes of the Supreme Essence, gods; and this word had been so commonly applied to a vast variety of superior intelligences, that it could not answer the Apostle's evident intention. He therefore formed a sentence, to express in the most emphatic manner, THE SUPREME GODHEAD OF CHRIST; so that both Jew and Gnostic might be sure of his intention and his meaning.

It is a poor effort to try to emasculate this text, by quoting Eph. 3 : 19, as is sometimes done: "And to know the love of Christ, which passeth knowledge, that ye might be filled with *all the fullness of God.*" The Apostle, in the context of this verse, had said that Jews and Gentiles were built up together into a holy *Temple*, and upon this metaphor he grafts his prayer, that this temple might be filled with all the fullness of God; that they might be a "holy temple for an habitation of God through the Spirit." This does not convey any idea like that in Col. 2 : 9, where the "fullness of the *God*HEAD" (divine nature) *really*, not metaphorically, is said to dwell in Christ. The original is σωματικῶς, *substantively*, v. 17, "They are a *shadow* (σκιά) of things to come, but the *substance* (σῶμα) is Christ."

Now, if Christ be not God, Paul is convicted of a deliberate intention, and of wicked craft, to lead men to regard Him as the Supreme. He is a *promoter* of idolatry, while he professes to detest it, and actually lampoons men for this stupid practice. We see no chance of escape from one or other of these alternatives. He has evidently so contrived his sentences, that they are *suggestive*, as well as expressive; and if this text does not teach the doctrine for which we contend, there is no meaning in language; and there is no possibility of telling the difference between the creature and the Creator!

(5.) 1 Cor. 15 : 47.—**The first man (Adam) is of the earth, earthy: the second *man* (Christ) is the *Lord from heaven*.**

In this text, the contrast is perfect. The second man, as to his manhood, must be *earthy* as well as the first, else he could not be man at all. Now, if the first be earthy, the second man is heavenly; but as this might be interpreted to mean a *holy disposition*, the term would not express the Apostle's idea, and he therefore said, that Christ was the *Lord from heaven*—a phrase wholly incompatible with the supposition that he is only a man or a creature. He is, indeed, expressly called a *man*. But if he be *only* a man, the contrast is ridiculous; for where is there a mere human being not of the earth? If he be an arch-*angel*, then there is just as much difficulty in admitting the union of the human and the angelic as there is in admitting the union of the human and the divine natures. Besides, how could any creature be called the "Lord from heaven"? This phrase is descriptive of the Supreme God. (Genesis 19 : 24; 2 Chron. 20 : 6.) 'Ο κύριος, The Lord, both in the Sept. and N. T. is the translation of "Jehovah." With the article, it generally means the Supreme God; (Matt. 1 : 22; 2 : 15; 5 : 33; Luke 1 : 6, 29; Mark 5 : 19; James 4 : 15;) but often it is without the article, being *defined* by something else in the sentence, (Acts 7 : 31;) and in this respect, it has the license of a proper name, either taking or rejecting the article at the pleasure of the writer. It smeaning here is put beyond dispute, because *defined* both by the article, and by the words, *from heaven*. Our Saviour said of himself: "He that cometh from above, is above all: he that is of the *earth is earthy*, and speaketh of the earth: he that cometh from heaven is above all." Doubtless, Paul had this in his mind, when he penned this verse; and must be understood as referring to the Divinity of our Lord, who, he says, is "over all, God blessed for ever." If this be not so, if the union between the human and divine natures in the person of our Redeemer is not here taught, then we despair of finding any sense in the passage.

(6.) 1 Tim. 1 : 1.—Paul, an apostle of Jesus Christ, by the commandment of *God* our Saviour, and *Lord* Jesus Christ, our hope.

If this verse mean any thing, it must mean that our hope rests on Jesus Christ, not only as man, but as *God* and *Lord.*

(7.) 1 Tim. 3 : 16.—Without controversy, great is the mystery of godliness. *God was manifest in the flesh,* justified in the Spirit, seen of angels, preached unto the Gentiles, believed on in the world, received up into glory.*

* We here subjoin a note on this passage by the Rev. Dr. Brownlee:

"The Alexandrian MS., and all known manuscripts, except two of the Palestine, and one of the Egyptian edition, read Θεος, God, in 1 Tim. 3 : 16. The Latin Vulgate reads 'quod' 'which,' in opposition to every known manuscript but the Clermont.—See Nolan's Inquiry into the Integrity of the Greek Vulgate, and received text of the New Testament, p. 285.

"Nolan reveals a fact of importance, in reference to the reading of the text. In the very ancient Alexandrian MS., the words have been much worn out; and hence, some critics, as Wetstein and Griesbach, following certain prejudices, declared that they read 'Ος, *which,* and not $\overline{\Theta\varsigma}$, which is the contraction of Θεος, God. On the other side, Junius, who *first* examined it, and Huish, and Bishops

We request the reader to turn back, and compare with this text, Rom. 9 : 5. The exposition there, sheds light upon 1 Tim. 3 : 16, for the same author penned both, and clearly conveys the same funda-

Walton and Fell, with Drs. Mill, Grabe, and Woide, declare that they read $\overline{\Theta}$ς, and not 'Oς; that is, they read 'GOD,' and not *which*. But Dr. Berriman has settled the point. In the presence of his two friends, Ridley and Gibson, he examined this ancient MS. in the sunshine, by the aid of a microscope. And he, and they, and two other persons standing by, saw distinctly the transverse line in the letter Θ; and therefore found it to be $\overline{\Theta}$ς, God; and not 'Oς, which. And a certificate was drawn up by Dr. B., and published in the following words: 'And therefore, if at any time, hereafter, the old line should become indiscernible, there never will be just cause to doubt, but that the genuine and original reading of this MS. is $\overline{\Theta}$ς, that is, Θεος, God.'

"And in reference to Wetstein, *whose single testimony* is now supposed to turn the scale against the above host of witnesses, Dr. Berriman publicly charged him with the fact of having *admitted* to a friend that *he saw the transverse line, and so read* $\overline{\Theta}$ς. But he afterwards disputed it. And Griesbach has followed in the same track. To this charge Wetstein replied, that in examining the MS., *he mistook the transverse line of an* E *on the other side of the vellum, which appeared through, and so deceived him into the idea, at first, that it was* $\overline{\Theta}$ς. This gross prevarication of Wetstein was promptly detected by Dr. Berriman, who again examined the MS., and found the letter E *so entirely distant from the word on the other side, that it could not have been mistaken, by any one, for the genuine transverse line in* $\overline{\Theta}$ς*!* Having thus settled the case with Wetstein, the learned Nolan proceeds to show the duplicity and unfairness of Griesbach in this matter.—See Nolan's Inquiry, etc., pp. 282, 285, 512, 513."

"See also his criticism on the ungrammatical phrase, *μυστηϱίον, ός*, etc.; and then the transition from *ός* into *ό*, in the neuter gender, to agree with the neuter noun. (Nolan pp. 281, 282.)"

Also, Dr. Henderson's volume on this text.

mental idea of two-fold nature in both. It appears to us, to require some courage to deny this; and it would appear our opponents think so too, if we may judge from the manner by which, in both instances, they try to support their denial. On the common interpretation, this text is plain, but if only a *man* was thus manifested, where is the mystery? How great the nonsense—"A man was manifested in the flesh;" if only a creature, how vast the confusion! By substituting "which," or "he who," for *God*, as is done by the Unitarians, the sense of the passage is completely destroyed.*

* The external evidence for Θεος, as given by Dr. Henderson, is overwhelming. The internal evidence is clearly in its favor. Neither *ὅς*, nor *ὁ* so well agrees with the context. Not to speak of unusual construction, they exceedingly embarass the sense. What can be the meaning of *ὅς ἐφανερώθη ἐν σαρκί*? Granting that, although unusual, it may be allowed on the ground of *anomaly*, what does it make Paul say, according to Unitarian faith? This: "Great is the mystery—*a man was manifest in the flesh*"! If Christ were only a man, there was no mystery in his appearance as such. He could appear no otherwise. If we may be allowed to judge from the writings of this Apostle, we must say, it was next to impossible that he should pen such a sentence. It is nowhere said, that "*Christ* was manifested in the flesh." The effort to make Χριστος the antecedent of *ὅς*, understood, is not only harsh and unnatural, but incapable of defense, either from parallel passages, or from Pauline usage, or from probability. Nor can it be said that *τὸ τῆς εὐσεβειας μυστήριον* is the antecedent, nor *ἐκκλησια θεοῦ*, for neither of them was *manifested in the flesh*. The nearest masculine antecedent is *θεοῦ ζῶντος*, but this will not suit the Unitarian at all; besides, it is too far from the relative. If the reading be 'O, then, although agreeing in gender with the nearest antecedent, it makes rank nonsense. The plea, therefore, that this passage is *disputed*, can

(8.) John 1 : 1, 2, 3, 14.—In the beginning was the WORD, and the WORD was with God, and the WORD was GOD. The same was in the beginning with God. All things were made by him, and without him was not any thing made that was made. In him was life: and the life was the light of men. And the Word was made flesh, and dwelt among us.

The term Word is evidently so applied in this passage, that it must mean either a creature or the Creator. If it be the latter, then the passage is intelligible; but if it mean the former, it is absurd. Supposing it means a creature, by substituting terms, we have the following instruction: "In the beginning was a *creature*, and a *creature* was with God, and a *creature* was God (!) The same (creature) was in the beginning with God. All things were made by a *creature*, and without a *creature* was not any thing made that was made." Of course, this creature *acted* before he *existed;* for his first *act* was to *make himself!* "And a creature was made flesh, and dwelt among us." If this creature was more than man, a subordinate God, then there are at least *two* Gods, contrary to 1 Cor. 8: 5, 6: "Though there be that are called gods, whether in heaven or in earth, to us there is but *one* God;" and Christianity is but a modified form of Polytheism; and if this creature was only a man, then it was deemed necessary for inspiration

not avail to drive it out of the discussion. In defense of the common reading, we refer to John 1 : 1, Θεὸς ἦν ὁ λογος; 14 v. *καὶ ὁ λόγος σὰρξ ἐγένετο·* 2 Cor. 5 : 19, Θεὸς ἦν ἐν Χριστῷ κόσμον καταλασσων εαυτῷ. These illustrate Θεὸς ἐφανερωθη ἐν σαρκί. See also, 1 John 1 : 2; Rom. 1 : 3; 8 : 3; 9 : 5.

to tell us, lest we should mistake, that *a man was made flesh!* These absurdities are truths, if Unitarianism be true.

In speaking of this passage, the author of the book entitled, "How I became a Unitarian," thus discourses, (p. 82:) "Now, if the Apostle means us to understand by the *Word*, or Logos, being made flesh, that God, the incomprehensible, the infinite and glorious Jehovah, was made flesh," etc., etc., "then upon the responsibility of my own judgment, and in the light of my own reason, and by virtue of that reverence for God" (rebellion against God?) "which is in me, I withdraw my credence entirely and unqualifiedly from this part of the narrative." This is a summary way of getting rid of strong proofs, but not very creditable either to the head or the heart of the writer. How much better to treat the whole Bible in the same way as the Deist does. He is as much at liberty to reject the whole, as Unitarians are to cut out a part, and certainly more consistent. We can not imagine greater inconsistency than to hold the Bible to be the word of God, and at the same time to avow such sentiments as the following, (pp. 159, 160:) "The writers of the New Testament were certainly in error respecting the approaching dissolution of the world. This is undeniable. Well, if they were mistaken in this instance, might they not have been in another? (namely, the doctrine of endless punishment.) If they were fallible men, laboring under the disadvantages of want of education, strong prejudices, and narrow Jewish sympathies, were they not likely to be bigoted in their notions, severe in their judgments of unbelievers, and rather free in their denunciations? This, from their own showing, was their character; and their writings confirm it. They were the very men to fulminate this dreadful doctrine. It was but the expression of their own tortured and exasperated feelings, wrung from them by the contempt, the hatred, the persecutions of their enemies. How could they think otherwise of those bloody-minded and ruthless men, who hunted, manacled, and slew them, than that they themselves would yet be devoured by an unquenchable flame? This was exceedingly natural."

Now we appeal to the common-sense of the world, to decide whether it be at all *rational* to treat the New Testament with any degree of respect as the word of God, if such traits of character may be fairly ascribed to the writers, and such motives assigned for the enunciation of their doctrines? This is, indeed, a sorry exhibit of "rational Christianity." But we take it as we find it in the language of a convert from "orthodoxy," rendering an account of himself: "How I became a Unitarian."

But lest we may be charged with doing this author injustice, we shall give what we understand to be his exposition of our passage, (p. 82:) "Like St. Paul, St. John had in view the preëxistent glory of Christ, as the first-born of every creature; or the Logos or Reason by which God had created the world." Again do we appeal to the common-sense of mankind, to decide whether it be more rational to accept the doctrine of Christ's two-fold nature, or to believe that the infinite Reason of Jehovah, John had in view as the first-born of every *creature.* We take it upon ourselves to say, it was impossible that John could have had any such view, because Christ said that the Spirit would guide him into *all truth.* (John 16 : 13.) Now, nothing can be more absurd that the supposition, that the Reason of the uncreated God, by which He made the world, was itself the first of the creation; and to present John as writing under this impression, is to present him as a fool, and his Master as at least forgetful of His promise.

Dr. Priestley, in hopes of augmenting his sect, addressed a publication to the Jews, telling them that, as he and those who thought with him had abandoned the doctrine of the Divinity of Jesus Christ, regarding him only as a mere man, there was nothing to prevent the Jews from becoming Christians upon the basis of Unitarianism. To this he received an answer, that it was impossible for the Jews ever to become Unitarians, since, if they were to receive the New Testament, they would have to acknowledge the doctrine of the Divinity of Christ, as plainly inculcated therein. The Jewish author of this answer, moreover, took the occasion to express his surprise, that Dr. P. could deny this doctrine, while he professed to acknowledge the authority of the New Testament. We think the Jew had a nicer perception of consistency than his celebrated correspondent. But the Musselman, Ameth Ben Ameth, ambassador from Morocco to the court of Charles II., treated the English Unitarians more unceremoniously, when they offered to unite with the Mohammedans, and tendered him their humble services in expurgating their Koran. He returned their communication without a reply. The Jew and the Mohammedan could appreciate this absurdity of Unitarianism—receiving the New Testament as the word of God, and at the same time denying one of its plainest and most important doctrines, with which its entire credit must stand or fall.*

(9.) Heb. 1, 2, 3.—God hath in these last days spoken unto us by his SON, *who is the brightness of his glory and the express image of his person.*

The original is much stronger than our translation. Here we have a definition of the *nature* of Christ, and the phraseology bears evidence of laboring thought. God's attributes are his glory, and his person means his nature. Now, he can not stamp his nature upon any creature, nor give his incommunicable attributes to another; yet Christ is here called the effulgence or lustre of God's glory. The "express image" means a stamp, as of a seal. The word translated "person" means an independent essence or being. Then the passage reads as follows: "God hath in these last days spoken unto us by his SON,

* See their proposed negotiation, in the Appendix.

who is the brightness of the divine glory, the *stamp or correspondence of God's essence.*" Can this be said of any creature? IT CAN NOT. In order to show the infinite love of our Maker, in sending us the *Messiah*, Paul directs us to his higher nature, which is the radiation of God's own attributes, and the engraving of his very being; and his language clearly implies its own inadequacy to *define* Christ. It is utterly and especially inconsistent in a prosaic, didactic essay, upon the supposition that He is only a creature.

(10.) Rev. 22 : 6, 16.—And he said unto me, These sayings are faithful and true: and THE LORD GOD OF THE HOLY PROPHETS sent HIS angel to show unto his servants the things which must shortly be done. . . . . I, JESUS, have sent MINE angel to testify unto you these things in the churches. I am the ROOT and OFFSPRING of David.

In both of these passages, the senders denote the same person; in both, the one sent is the same; and the language of both, by mutual illustration, clearly decide that Jesus is the LORD GOD. On any other interpretation than that which harmonizes these passages, by the doctrine of the two-fold nature in Christ, we should be glad to know how the metaphor can be justified, which makes both the ROOT and SHOOT of David representatives of Christ.

(11.) Tit. 2 : 13.—Looking for that blessed hope, and the glorious appearing of the GREAT GOD AND (EVEN) OUR SAVIOUR JESUS CHRIST.

Προσδεχόμενοι τὴν μακαρίαν ἐλπίδα, καὶ ἐπιφάνειαν τῆς δόξης τȣ͂ μεγάλου Θεοῦ καὶ σωτῆρος ἡμῶν Ἰησου Χριστοῦ.

According to the usual idiom of the Greek language, referred to in the note below,* the article

* The Greek Article.—Learned men have submitted to patient labor and wearisome research, to ascertain the precise force of the Greek article, which is always *definite*. Middleton and Sharp have stated the *general rule;* and thinking they had materials enough to warrant it, they dogmatized in very positive language: but others have discovered a multitude of exceptions, which compel us to be cautious in its application.

The Rule which applies to the construction of these and similar texts in the original Greek is this:

"When two or more personal nouns, of the same gender, number and case, are coupled together by the conjunction *καὶ*, and the article is prefixed to the *first*, but not to the *second*, *third*, etc., those two or more nouns, whether they be substantives or adjectives, denote *one* and the *same person*. This is the case also when two *participles* are thus coupled together."

In support of this rule are cited many passages from the Scriptures, the fathers, and profane writers, in which it is impossible, it is said, to mistake its application.

Examples. Matt. 12 : 22. *ὥστε τὸν τυφλὸν καὶ κωφὸν καὶ λαλεῖν καὶ βλέπειν.*

Acts 3 : 14. *Ὑμεῖς δὲ τὸν ἅγιον καὶ δίκαιον ἠρνησασθε.*

John 11 : 26. *Καὶ πᾶς ὁ ζῶν καὶ πιστεύων εἰς ἐμὲ, οὐ μὴ ἀποθάνῃ εἰς τὸν αἰῶνα.*

2 Cor. 1 : 3. *Εὐλογητὸς ὁ Θεὸς καὶ πατὴρ τοῦ Κυρίου ἡμῶν Ἰησοῦ Χριστοῦ, ὁ πατὴρ τῶν οἰκτιρμῶν, καὶ Θεὸς πασης παρακλήσεως,* (two examples in this verse.)

See original of 2 Cor. 11 : 31; Heb. 3 : 1; Phil. 4 : 20; Col. 2 : 2; 2 Pet. 2 : 20; Rev. 16 : 15; Eph. 6 : 21; James 1 : 27.

Though it be true that a noun without the article is subjected to that of the preceding noun connected with it, yet this is not always the case. Sometimes a genitive, following the second noun, contains definition enough in itself, to warrant the omission of repeating the article.

expressed before the *first* and omitted before the *second* of two nouns of the same case, connected by the copulative *καὶ*, *defines* both alike. To this general.rule there are many exceptions; but when any other *defining* word occurs in the sentence applicable to both nouns thus connected, the force of the article over the second can not be questioned. Now, to prove our text safe from any argument founded on exceptions to this rule, we have two remarks to make:

1. The pronoun OUR, may belong to and define both nouns, God and Saviour; thus the literal rendering is: "Looking for the blessed hope, even the appearing of the glory of the Great God and Saviour OF US, Jesus Christ."

2. What renders this application of the pronoun certain, is the word *appearing*, which further defines both nouns alike. There can be no mistake here.

Again: When two nouns are coupled after the article, they may denote things *closely related*, but not *absolutely identical*. See original of Mark 11 : 15; 15 : 1; Eph. 2 : 20.

Hence, in appealing to the original, in this discussion, for an argument, we must not rely, in the first instance, so much on the general rule *per se*, as upon other qualifying and defining words, whose precision shall show our texts *must* be construed in accordance with it.

There are two ways in which a noun may be made *definite*. First, by the article, designating some kind of definiteness. Second, by the addition of some qualifying term or circumstance, serving to make it definite, in which case the article may or may not be employed. But when the article is helped, by the defining power of other words in a sentence, we can then build an argument of some value upon the idiom we discuss, such as the one designated in the aforesaid canon.

But where, in all the Scriptures, is the Great God said to appear? Nowhere. The contrary is the affirmation. "No man hath seen God at any time." "He dwelleth in light which no man can approach unto, whom no man hath seen or can see." No created eye can penetrate the enveloping glory of his awful majesty, and gaze upon him. When Moses made the bold request: "I beseech thee, show me thy glory," the response for ever settled the matter. "Thou canst not see my face, for there shall no man see me and live." Yet in our text, the blessed hope is said to be, the *appearing of the Great God.* Paul well knew that He is *invisible* as well as immortal, and therefore expounded his meaning by the additional clause, "and Saviour of us, Jesus Christ." Now this important word, *appearing,* is used in various passages to denote the second coming of our Lord. 2 Thes. 2 : 8, "Whom the Lord shall consume with the spirit (breath) of his mouth, and shall destroy with the brightness (appearance) of his coming." 1 Tim. 6 : 14, "Until the appearing of our Lord Jesus Christ." 2 Tim. 1 : 10, "By the *appearing* of our Saviour Jesus Christ;" v. 8, "Unto all that love his appearing." Here, then, we have the force of this noun, giving certainty to our application of the pronoun, and both showing that our text must be interpreted by the general rule aforesaid. Thus we read, "Looking for the blessed hope, even the appearing of OUR GREAT GOD AND SAVIOUR, JESUS CHRIST." Nothing need be more satisfactory. We exhibit it as the keen blade that severs every sinew of the Socinian heresy. It can not be managed by Unitarians in any other way than that of *torture* by means of Dr. Channing's rule of exegesis; by which they "*do not hesitate to modify, and restrain, and turn from their most obvious sense,*" all texts like this.

It is perfectly plain that Paul here meant to describe Christ as the Great God, for he so constructed his sentence, that by an article, pronoun, and noun, he should prevent all mistake, since their combined force clearly shows that the nouns *God* and *Saviour*, are shut up to the operation of the general rule. Hence it is clear that he meant to say, Christ is the Great God; or he meant to use a Greek idiom pointedly, for the purpose of deception. There is no avoiding this, because Paul was a scholar, and well knew the force of his own words.

(12.) 2 Pet. 1 : 1. **To them that have obtained like precious faith with us through (in) the righteousness of God and (even) our Saviour Jesus Christ.**

τοῖς ἰσότιμον ἡμῖν λαχοῦσι πίστιν ἐν δικαιοσύνῃ τον Θεοῦ ἡμῶν καὶ σωτῆρος Ἰησου Χριστοῦ·

The *second* noun (*σωτῆρος*) being without the article, is *defined* by that of the *first* of the two united by *και*, according to usage. To show this text safe from all arguments from exceptions to the rule referred to, we remark that *ἡμῶν* defines both nouns. Thus, literally "faith in the righteousness of the God of us and Saviour Jesus Christ." Precisely the same construction occurs in 2 Pet. 3 : 18. "The knowledge of the Lord of us and Saviour Jesus Christ." That the word "Saviour" here is explicative of "Lord," both belonging to Christ, will not be questioned. The same order of words occurs in 2 Pet. 1 : 11, and in other places. So that the influence of the genitive, as seen in these examples which might easily be multiplied, brings our text under the general rule, and we read, "faith in the righteousness of OUR GOD AND SAVIOUR JESUS CHRIST."

The word *righteousness* belongs to both nouns. Christ is the procuring cause of righteousness to us. (Jer. 23 : 5, 6; Dan. 9 : 24; Rom. 5 : 17, 18; 1 Cor. 1 : 30.) This is called the *righteousness of faith*, (Rom. 10 : 4–10;) and does not refer to the personal quality of rectitude in Deity, (Phil. 3 : 9,) but to the method of justification of the soul by Christ. But Peter writes to those who "have obtained like precious faith in the righteousness of our *God* and Saviour." It is therefore clear that this text is shut up to the operation of the general rule which makes the words "Saviour Jesus Christ" an explanation of *our God.* That which is the great object of precious faith, is the method of justification of which *our God and Saviour* is the author.

(13.) Jude 4.—Denying the ONLY LORD GOD, AND (even) OUR LORD JESUS CHRIST.

καὶ τὸν μόνον δεσπότην Θεὸν καὶ Κύριον ἡμῶν 'Ιησȣν Χριστὸν ἀρνούμενοι.

(Literally)—"Denying the only Master God and Lord of us, Jesus Christ." Here also the general rule applies, but other considerations help to prove that the Apostle referred the three appellatives to Christ: 1. δεσπότης is a term applied both to the Father and the Son. 2 Pet. 2 : 1, δεσπότην ἀρνούμενοι, (same word used here,) without doubt applies to Christ. (2 Tim. 2 : 21.) In Acts 4 : 24; Rev. 6 : 10, it is applied to God the Father.

Again. *Denying* Christ=rejecting him, is a New-Testament idiom. (Mat. 26 : 34, 35; Mark 14 : 30, 31, 72; Luke 12 : 9; John 13 : 18; Acts 3 : 13, 14; 2 Tim. 2 : 12; 1 John 2 : 22, 23.) Hence it appears, that the application of the article here is in accordance with the idiom of the Greek language, which makes GOD AND LORD JESUS CHRIST *explanatory* of OUR MASTER: and this is put beyond a reasonable doubt, by the use of the same words in other passages where their application is clearly made to Christ. Therefore "the only Master of us is Jesus Christ our GOD AND LORD."

We may now appeal to any unprejudiced mind whether there be any truth in the following statements.

*"In the New Testament there are a considerable number of titles and epithets and attributes applied or ascribed to the Supreme Being which can not be clearly shown to have been used in any passage, respecting our Lord and Saviour Jesus Christ." "There is not one clear instance in which *Jehovah*,

* "Scripture Proofs of Unitarianism," pp. 178, 179.

the hallowed name of the self-existent Deity, is applied in Holy Writ to Jesus of Nazareth." "It is highly probable that there are not more than four instances of the application of the term *God* to Christ, in the whole compass of the sacred volume." These four, we presume, are thought to be nicely disposed of by the operation of Dr. Channing's rule of exegesis. "In no instance did the Lord Jesus ever assume a higher title than that of *the Son of God.*" "The titles and appellations by which Jesus generally distinguished himself or was distinguished by his primitive disciples and others, do not indicate a truly divine nature." "On no occasion did our Lord claim any of the incommunicable attributes of Deity."

We think, it will appear, from our proofs, that this author has been excessively rash in making these assertions. We have shown that κυρίος is the translation of *Jehovah;* and when Thomas exclaimed, "My Lord and my God," he either applied the title Jehovah to Christ in its usual Old-Testament combination, or he was guilty of swearing. We have given an "instance" of Christ's assuming the high title of "King of kings and Lord of lords," and also, an instance where he claimed omniscience, as "the Searcher of hearts." The aforesaid assertions are not therefore trustworthy, and it was indeed a bold presumption to venture such language. We believe it entirely unwarranted, and if we mistake not, the most of men, who will weigh our arguments, will pass the same judgment.

We have now given twenty-five instances of *inspired commentary*, in some of which the commentators distinctly tell us they apply their quotations from the Old Testament, according to the *original* intention of the prophets; and thirteen didactic passages taken out of the New Testament, descriptive of Christ. Now let us look at them in their collective strength, and then determine whether they can be applied to Christ at all, if he be but a *creature.*

JEHOVAH—THE MOST HIGH GOD—THE SEARCHER OF HEARTS—GOD—LORD—JEHOVAH GOD OF TRUTH—THE KING JEHOVAH OF HOSTS—JEHOVAH OF HOSTS HIMSELF—OUR GOD—JEHOVAH GOD—THE FIRST AND THE LAST—BESIDES WHOM NO GOD—THE STRONG JEHOVAH—ALMIGHTY—EVERLASTING RULER—WONDERFUL—COUNSELLOR—THE MIGHTY GOD—THE EVERLASTING FATHER—THE PRINCE OF PEACE—THE WORD WHO WAS GOD—GOD OVER ALL—THE EQUAL WITH GOD—THE REAL FULLNESS OF THE GODHEAD—THE LORD FROM HEAVEN—GOD MANIFEST IN THE FLESH—THE GREAT GOD—THE STAMP OF GOD'S ESSENCE—GOD AND LORD—GOD OUR SAVIOUR—THE TRUE GOD—ETERNAL LIFE—THE ONLY WISE GOD—

THE KING OF KINGS AND LORD OF LORDS —THE LORD GOD OF THE HOLY PROPHETS.

Here are thirty-five appellatives in all varieties of combination, expressive of the *existence*, and explanatory of the *nature* and *attributes* of the Supreme Being, applied to Christ; and it would seem, so as to prevent any mistake. Had the intention of the sacred writers been to present the doctrine of the Divinity of Christ, as the only prominent doctrine of the Gospel, they might have used these terms more frequently, but we are sure they could not have used stronger language. Now we may ask, will any man in his senses, after a fair view of the subject, suppose that these sublime and divine titles, by any possibility can be applied as descriptive of a CREATURE? We are sure they can not, without the grossest blasphemy. Thus did the Eternal announce himself to Isaiah: "I am Jehovah, *that is my name*, and my glory will I not give unto another." Yet with this familiar text upon their hearts as Jews, did the New-Testament writers not only ascribe the peculiar name of Jehovah to Christ, but also that name in every form and combination that can convey the idea of Supreme Godhead! What, then, is the consequence? THIS. Either Christ is God, or the whole Bible is a delusion! Either Christ is God, or the Apostles are gross deceivers! If they have interpreted the sacred oracles *rightly*, then the Prophets have been the most wicked men that ever lived; and if the prophets are to be believed, then God is the AUTHOR OF SIN!! *

This is an awful conclusion, but from it there is no *escape*. If Christ be God, all the animated, glowing descriptions of prophecy, all these divine titles are his by *right;* and the writers very properly go the whole length of language in the very combination of words that must necessarily express supreme Godhead. But if Christ be not God, the Apostles apply terms and phrases to him which can never be given to any created being without blasphemy. No creature in heaven or earth, was ever honored with such divine titles. If they correctly quote the prophets, *these* also are involved in the same condemnation; and if the prophets "spake as they were moved by the Holy Ghost," then God, who most severely punished men for idolatry, himself inspired the writer of the entire Bible to lead men into that abominable sin which he hates!! Such are the consequences that flow from the denial of the doctrine

* Unitarian writers sometimes come very near charging moral evil upon their Maker. The author of "How I became a Unitarian," goes so far as to say that the existence of it "implicates him in so far as to authorize us to look to him for something by which it shall be finally extinguished, and its consequences averted from those who now suffer from it. It is a sound maxim in law, that he who does a particular action by means of another, does it himself, *qui facit per alium, facit per se.* He does not do it personally, but is morally and legally responsible for it." "I believe that God is bound by every moral attribute of his character to rescue himself from the cruel suspicion the presence of this evil seems to imply." !!!

in question. And that what we have just stated as logical conclusions, by fair deduction is not misstated, we are willing to leave to the judgment of our candid readers.

Between God and the super-archangel of Arian conception, there must be an infinite distance; yet every word used to describe the Supreme God, is also used to describe Christ. They, then, who affirm that man or angel or any creature may receive even a tithe of these distinctive names of the Infinite Being are reduced to this dilemma—

Either they must deny that the Supreme God has any peculiar name at all, by which he can be distinguished from his creatures, or they must admit that Christ is the SUPREME GOD.

They must take their choice in view of what Christ himself says: "If ye believe not that I AM HE, ye shall die in your sins—and whither I go ye can not come." All men must admit that the proposition—God has *no* peculiar name to distinguish him from his creatures—is sufficiently absurd, but *every* name by which our Maker is known is directly applied to Christ. Therefore he is THE SUPREME GOD.

CHAPTER III.

II. DILEMMA.—*Either Christ is God, or Mohammed has given more correct ideas of God, and is therefore a safer guide than Jesus of Nazareth.*

Christ's conduct—Asserts his claim before the Jews—Explains his nature to Philip—Quotations from the Koran—Dilemma verified—Unitarian explanation.

PAUL has represented God, as having, last of all, spoken to us by his Son. In order, then to ascertain the claims of Christ, and how he has taught us to regard the Deity, we must examine his own words on these subjects.

All readers of the New Testament must have observed that our Saviour was sparing of open declarations as to his person and his claims. He preferred to leave the people to their own reflections. They had the Scriptures which "testified of him," and they needed no help to draw inferences from his character, his instructions, and his mighty works. There was an obvious propriety in this course. Taking the advantage of prevalent opinion as to the fulfillment of prophecy, many false Messiahs already had appeared; and each did precisely what we should expect impostors to do, namely, issue proclamation of His coming, "to whom the gathering of the nations should be;" and with outspoken asseverations, lay claim to the Messianic character, and to an acknowledgment of the same by the people. But when the true Christ came, the way was *prepared* for him by his forerunner; and he preferred to justify the high expectations raised by John, by more than meeting them; so that their own inferences should lead the people to the conviction, that he was "the consolation of Israel;" and to seek from himself a decision upon this point, then agitating the whole Jewish world.

Many were forced into the belief that he was the Messiah from his words, and works; and accordingly so declared for him; public opinion was fast forming in his favor, and the leaders of the Jews, having from the first, contracted strong prejudices against him, found it necessary to turn the current, which if unchecked, might cause them to lose, "both their place and nation." Hence they sought earnestly to make our Lord commit himself in controversy, that they might have some pretext for the execution of their base design. Let us now see what Christ says of himself.

We open the New Testament at the place where the Jews quarreled with him, and sought to kill him mainly for this crime, that *he made himself equal with God.* In his controversy with them on this occasion, he used the following words:

John 5 : 23.—All men should honor the Son, EVEN AS they honor the Father. He that honoreth not the Son, honoreth not the Father, which hath sent him.

Such is the declaration of Jesus Christ, in reference to the character he claimed. What is this character? The Jews understood him to make himself *equal* with God, and he knew it; but did not correct them for misapprehension of his words. How then are we to *honor* him? Are we to consider him equal with, or inferior to the Father? Must we pay him divine homage, or only honor him with a less esteem? These are important questions, and we believe there need be no difficulty in settling this point. Upon the supposition that Christ meant to claim Supreme Godhead, the rule of duty could not be more explicitly laid down. We are to honor the Son EVEN AS, or in the same way, to the same extent, as the Father; "χαθὼς, *in the manner that* they honor the Father." Now we all agree that no one honors the Father at all, unless he worship him as the Supreme God. To him we owe the highest act of divine honor, and if we must honor the *Son* "even as" the Father, it appears to us that the matter is decided. We must worship Christ even as the Supreme God. But he that pays the highest act of divine worship to a being *inferior* to God, breaks the first command, and he that breaks the first command, violates the whole law, and he that violates the law, is worthy of death. Christ came to "magnify the law and make it honorable," but if He be not the Supreme God, then he taught all men how to *defeat* the very end, for which he himself came into the world! He that worshippeth not the Father, worshippeth not God; he that worshippeth not the Son, worshippeth not the Father, therefore, whoever worshippeth not the Son, worshippeth not God. If we would worship HIM aright, according to this text, we must render equal honor to the Father and the Son; but *equal* honor supposes *equal* dignity, and in order to render the one, we must believe the other. We can not, therefore, see how the conclusion is to be avoided, that whoever does not worship the Son, as profoundly as he worships the Father, does not worship God at all.

It becomes us, then, to count the cost of living without an intimate acquaintance with *the truth as it is in Jesus.* Now, there are various kinds of truth, all of which are important; but there is only *one* which has a direct practical bearing upon our future condition. Christ said, "I am THE TRUTH;" and it is for our highest interest to know what is meant by "the truth as it IS in Jesus." We think it means, not only the system of facts and doctrines in the Bible, but also the wonderful constitution of our Mediator, in his two-fold nature, which presents the most stupendous fact, and the most glorious doctrine of THE TRUTH. In this matter, above all others, *indifference* is *criminality.*

Now, it can not be pretended that our Saviour claimed simply, that honor "which according to the custom of the age and of the eastern world, was paid to men invested with great authority, whether in civil or religious concerns;" for he was invested with nothing of this kind by the dignitaries of either Church or State. His authority was that of God, and he so strongly asserted it, that he was adjudged a blasphemer for making himself *equal* with God; and instead of preventing or removing this impression which he had made, he actually *confirmed* it by claiming such an *honor* as is *equal* to, or the same as, Divine adoration. Yet we are told, by an author already referred to, "that Christ never spoke of himself as an object of worship"!

John 10 : 30-33. On a subsequent occasion when "the Jews came round about him, and said unto him, How long dost thou make us to doubt?" Christ said in his reply: "I AND MY FATHER ARE ONE." For this assertion they again attempted to stone him, and when he remonstrated, they thus justified themselves: "For a good work we stone thee not; but for blasphemy; and because that thou, being *a man*, makest thyself *God*." Now, if Christ were only a man, if he were only a creature, the Jews acted perfectly right; and he knew they were acting according to the requirement of their law; but because he did not disclaim, because he did not correct their mistake, it follows that Christ is God, and as such, must claim divine worship. We agree with Dr. Channing in the belief, that "it is impossible that a teacher of infinite wisdom should expose those whom he would teach to infinite error." Therefore we argue that Christ must be God. No man can get rid of the fact that he made an impression upon the Jews, which led them to suppose him guilty of the very crime for which they sought to kill him. Did not Christ, then, "expose them to infinite error," by making, and then confirming this impression? And on the supposition of his being but a man, can he be acquitted of dishonesty, and the most enormous wickedness? Never. Now let us retire with him and his disciples, and hear what he has to say of himself in private.

John 14 : 7-10.—Christ made this reply to enlighten his disciples on the very matter now in dispute: "If ye had known me, ye should have known my Father also: and from henceforth ye know him, and have seen him. Philip saith unto him, Lord, *show* us the *Father*, and it *sufficeth* us. Jesus saith unto him: Have *I* been so long time with you, and yet hast thou not known *me*, Philip? He that hath seen *me*, hath seen the *Father:* and how sayest thou then, Show us the Father? Believest thou not that I am in the Father, and the Father in me? The words that I speak unto you, I speak not of myself, but the Father that dwelleth in me, he doeth the work."

Without entering into a critical analysis of this passage, it is perfectly plain that the language conveys something essentially different from, and infinitely beyond, mere unity of purpose and will. There is no question as to the meaning of the term *Father:* all agree that the Supreme God is the great subject of discourse. It can not be denied. Let us then substitute one term for the other, and read the luminous declaration: "If ye had known me, ye should have known *God* also, and (but) from henceforth ye know him, and have seen him. Philip saith unto him: Lord, show us *God*, and it sufficeth us. Jesus saith unto him: Have I been so long time with you, and yet hast thou not known *me*, Philip? He that has seen *me*, hath seen *God;* and how sayest thou show us *God?* Believest thou not that I am *in* God and God *in* me? The words that I speak unto you, I speak not of myself, but *God* that *dwelleth* in me, he doeth the work." Can this language, under any circumstances, be affirmed of himself by any creature? Never; the brightest seraph dare not say: "He that hath seen me, hath seen the Supreme God." It would be a blasphemous falsehood, it would be identifying the creature with the Creator.

Besides, Philip was making the same request that Moses made in Ex. 33 : 18, and our Lord proceeded to enlighten him on the subject of that request. But if Christ be simply a *creature*, what confusion could be more confounding than this: "He that hath seen me the creature, hath seen God the Creator. Believest thou not that I, the creature, am *in* God the Creator, and God the Creator, *in* me the creature?" Such language in the mouth of Him who was Philip's instructor, on the supposition that he is not the Supreme God, is, to say the least, the language of evasion and deception! He affirmed an essential untruth, and was guilty of the most horrid impiety, in arrogating to himself a divine nature, divine attributes, and divine honors, only to *deceive* the confidence of a simple inquirer after truth. He affirmed that to know Christ, and to know God; to see Christ, and to see God, was *one and the same thing*, because Christ was in God, and God was in Christ. Can language be stronger than this? Could any creature use it and be guiltless? No. What, then, is the conclusion to which we must come? If Christ be not God, if he be only a creature, he was dishonest with his poor disciple, he imposed upon his credulity an argument for his enlightenment, that could only perplex and mislead him. He taught him to regard a creature worthy of equal honor with the Almighty Father, after whom he was inquiring, and consequently presented himself as entitled to divine worship! How different the good Mohammed! What a perfect contrast between the prophet of Mecca, and the impostor of Galilee! The former declared that, "There is one God, and Mohammed is his prophet," but the latter, the more impious of the two, affirmed that he, a creature, was *in* the Creator, and the Creator *in* him, the creature!

How much more truthful the representation given by Mohammed! "Verily, the likeness of Jesus in the sight of GOD is as the likeness of Adam; He created him out of the dust, and then said unto him, Be; and he was." "Christ the son of Mary is no more than an Apostle, *other* Apostles have preceded him." "Jesus is no other than a servant, whom we favored *with the gift of prophecy.*"* This language is intelligible, precise, and can not be mistaken. Now, if Christ be not God, then it follows that the Prophet of Mecca was much better qualified to use language correctly than Christ, and was not guilty of making such perplexing explanations. *Mohammed* has more accurately described his nature than Christ's own *inspired witnesses.* In evidence of this, again we quote the Koran: "They are infidels who declare that God is Christ: Christ the son of Mary is no more than God's envoy. Christians say Christ is the Son of God; how are they infatuated! far be it from God that he should have *a Son.* Jesus is no other than a *servant.* O Jesus, son of Mary, dost thou persuade mankind to put thee in the place of God?"

It follows, therefore, that *Mohammed was more successful than Christ in giving right ideas of the great God, and of course is a safer guide than Jesus of Nazareth.*

It follows, that the disciples of the Crescent are the "true worshippers," and the children of wisdom; whilst those of the Cross are gross idolaters, and under the ban of their Maker! Escape this, who can.

Let us see how they succeed, who try to escape. The anonymous clergyman aforesaid, in his book entitled, "How I became a Unitarian," proceeds to say, (page 77,) that this passage, (John 14 : 7–10:) "Literally interpreted, forms the basis of a very strong argument on the Trinitarian side. It would be un-

* Sale's Koran, pp. 43, 92, 400.

fair to pass it." After perusing sundry observations preliminary to his "remarking upon these words," we were preparing ourselves for nothing less than an attempt at exposition; but how great was our astonishment when we had ended the following paragraph, (p. 80:) "We must take into consideration the undeniable fact, that the writer of this gospel was very much of a mystic, and that in him the spirit of exaggeration was large. He says at the close of his narrative: 'And there are also many other things which Jesus did, the which, if they should be written every one, I suppose that even the world itself could not contain the books that should be written.' So he delights in making (!) Jesus say: 'My flesh is meat indeed, and my blood is drink indeed,' etc. Hence if we accept the words first quoted—'He that hath seen me, hath seen the Father'—as a literal report of the conversation of Jesus, we should be doing that man of humble manners, meek and lowly at heart, a great wrong, to suppose that he meant to draw to himself the worship and adoration that were due to the Father alone. We must regard the passage as presenting us with something like a myth, in which the lower sense is made to assume the character of the higher: as when we speak of nature doing that which God alone can do, and thus by a change of terms, put nature in the place of God." In other words, courteous reader, John, the Beloved Disciple, *penned a falsehood!* No such conversation as he reports, literally took place! This is Unitarian exposition! Christ must have surely made a great mistake in selecting John and Paul for his "witnesses," and this, by the way, is an additional weight to their argument against his divinity!

CHAPTER IV.

III. DILEMMA: *Either Christ is God, or the Supreme Being has no incommunicable attribute peculiar to His nature, whereby he can be distinguished from His creatures.*

Eternity — Immutability — Omnipresence — Omnipotence — Omniscience—Immensity—Dilemma verified.

THE NATURE of the Creator must be essentially different from all the natures he has made. But wherein does this difference consist? Not only in his being, but in his attributes. These are communicable and incommunicable. The former he can give, the latter he can not give to his creatures. Reason, wisdom, and power, are attributes of God with which he has invested both the angelic and the human natures. But there is another class of perfections which, with reverence be it stated, he can not communicate. In making this assertion, we do not conceive ourselves as limiting the Holy One of Israel. There must be distinguishing properties that belong to God *alone*, such as man nor angel under any circumstances can receive. God, for instance, is everlasting, and necessarily independent; but Omnipotence himself can not make any creature possessing the attributes of eternity and independence, nor give *necessity* to his existence. A contrary supposition implies a contradiction. God is an Omnipotent, Omniscient, and Omnipresent Being, but he can not communicate these attributes to any creature. A contrary supposition involves an absurdity.

Now if it be found that Christ has *all these attributes* ascribed to him by the Records of Inspiration, then it must follow that he is the Supreme God. Let us see.

"Search the Scriptures," said our Redeemer, "they are they which testify of me." Here we shall make another collation from their contents, which will, we think, satisfactorily prove that the incommunicable attributes of Deity are ascribed to Christ.

1. *Eternity.* Micah 5 : 2.—But thou, Bethlehem Ephrata, though thou be little among the thousands of Judah, yet out of thee shall *He* come forth unto me that is to be ruler in Israel; whose goings forth have been of *old*, from *everlasting*.

Matt. 2 : 4–6.—He (Herod) demanded of them (the Jews) where Christ should be born, and they said unto him, In Bethlehem of Judea, for thus it is written by the prophet, And thou Bethlehem in the land of Juda, art not the least among the princes, for out of thee shall come a governor that shall rule my people Israel.

They evidently quoted from memory, but were sufficiently accurate to answer the question of Herod. That the prophecy referred to Christ, is clear enough from the fact that Christ was born in Bethlehem. Now the prophet says of him who was to be born at that place, that his goings forth have been of *old*, (from the beginning,) from *everlasting.* Christ is therefore possessed of this attribute of the Deity which can not possibly belong to the most exalted creature that God ever made.

Ex. 3 : 14.—And God said unto Moses, I AM THAT I AM : and he said, Thus shalt thou say unto the children of Israel, I AM hath sent me unto you.

John 8 : 58.—Jesus said unto them, Verily, verily I say unto you, before Abraham was, I AM.

The Jews took up stones to stone him, for blasphemy, for the reason assigned by them on another occasion : "Because thou being a man, makest thyself God." He did not correct them, as he doubtless would have done, had they misunderstood his words.

John 17 : 5.—Glorify me with the glory which I had with thee *before the world was.*

Col. 1 : 17.—*He is before all things.*

The words of Christ are put beyond dispute by the words of the Apostle. See the last example in our first collation. Moreover, Paul makes Melchisideck the type, and Christ the antitype. Heb. 7 : 3. Now a type must answer to its antitype in some prominent points of resemblance. Of Melchisideck, he says: "He had neither beginning of days nor end of life." What these words mean, it is not our business now to inquire, but the point of resemblance must be, the *eternity* of the antitype.

2. *Immutability.* Ps. 2 : 27.—But thou art the *same,* and thy years shall have no end.

Heb. 13 : 8.—Jesus Christ the *same* yesterday, to-day, and for ever.

In Heb. 1 : 12, Paul uses the words of David in the psalm just named, and descriptive of Jehovah, to describe Christ; but these words set forth the divine attribute of immutability; therefore, in Heb. 13 : 8, immutability is ascribed to Christ.

3. *Omnipresence.* Ex. 20 : 24.—In all places where I record my name I will come unto thee and will bless thee.

Matt. 18 : 20.—Where two or three are gathered together in my name, there am I in the midst of them.

The first of these passages is spoken of Jehovah, and refers to his omnipresence; the second, as to meaning, is identical with the first, and this attribute was therefore claimed by Christ.

John 3 : 13.—No man hath ascended up to heaven, but He that came down from heaven, even the Son of man which *is in heaven.*

But when Christ said this, he was *on earth* conversing with Nicodemus. How, then, could he be at the *same time* in heaven, unless omnipresence were an attribute of his person? How could he otherwise fulfill his own promise: "Lo, I am with you alway, even to the end of the world"?

4. *Omnipotence.* Jeremiah 27 : 5.—I have made the earth, the man and the beast that are upon the ground, by my great power, and by my outstretched arm, and have given it unto whom it seemed meet unto me.

John 5 : 19.—*Whatsoever* things the Father doeth, *these* also doeth the Son likewise.

The same extent of power is claimed in both quotations. Now, if the works of God prove him omnipotent, must not the same works prove Christ omnipotent? Surely. Therefore Paul argues, He "is able to do exceeding abundantly above all that we ask or THINK." (Eph. 3 : 20.)

5. *Omniscience.* 1 Kings 8 : 39.—Thou, even thou ONLY, knowest the hearts of the children of men.

John 2 : 24, 25.—But Jesus did not commit himself unto them, because he KNEW ALL MEN; and needed not that any should testify to him of man: for he KNEW WHAT WAS IN MAN.

Rev. 2 : 23.—Christ declares: "All the churches shall know that I AM HE WHO SEARCHETH the reins and hearts."

Nothing can be clearer than this. If omniscience belong not to Christ, then these passages can not be reconciled; if it do, then he is God. Therefore Paul's affirmation is true: "In him are hid *all the treasures of wisdom and knowledge.*"

6. *Immensity.* Jer. 23 : 24.—Do not I *fill* heaven and earth saith the Lord? (Jehovah.)

Eph. 1 : 23.—Christ "*filleth all in all.*"

What is claimed for Jehovah in the first quotation is claimed for Christ in the second; but that is immensity: therefore this divine attribute belongs to our Redeemer God.

Now, let us collect together these incommunicable attributes of Deity. It can not but be plain, that they are all appropriated to Christ. He is, then, the possessor of

ETERNITY—IMMUTABILITY—INDEPENDENCE—IMMENSITY—OMNIPOTENCE—OMNISCIENCE—OMNIPRESENCE.

Beyond a doubt these can never be communicated

to any mere creature, and, if the Scriptures are true, beyond a reasonable doubt they all belong to CHRIST. He therefore must be the SUPREME GOD. They who deny it, are reduced to this dilemma:

Either the Supreme God has NO *incommunicable attribute to distinguish the Divine from the human or angelic nature—or Christ is that Being!*

CHAPTER V.

IV. DILEMMA: *Either Christ is God, or, the truth of Scripture admitted, there is no proof that there is a God at all.*

Proof of the Divine existence appealed to by God himself—Collation of Scripture—an absurd consequence—Dilemma verified.

THE works of God, which, by his own authority, are the preëminent proofs of his existence and supremacy, are CREATION and PROVIDENCE. These are appealed to *by himself* as the most direct and positive evidence of both. "I am Jehovah that maketh all things." "To whom then will ye liken me, or shall I be equal? saith the Holy One. Lift up your eyes on high, and behold who hath created these things, that bringeth out their hosts by number: he calleth them all by names, by the greatness of his might, for that he is strong in power; not one faileth." (Is. 40 : 25, 26.) "Hast thou not known, hast thou not heard, that the everlasting God, Jehovah the Creator of the ends of the earth, fainteth not, neither is weary?" (28th v.) Thus the great argument which God uses in behalf of himself, constantly points us to his works of creation and providence; and thus instructed, Paul urges the inexcusableness of the heathen on this ground: "The invisible things of

Him from the creation of the world are clearly seen, being understood by the things that are made, even his eternal power and Godhead; so that they are without excuse." (Rom. 1 : 20.) The works of creation and providence therefore afford the GREATEST PROOF in natural and revealed religion of God's existence. Now, we think we can show that the same proof is available for the establishment of the Divinity of Christ. If we succeed in this, then the alternatives are, faith in the Supreme Godhead of our Redeemer, and BLANK ATHEISM. On the principles of right reason, there is no intermediate resting place, provided we admit the truth of Scripture, in which a consistent mind can find refuge. And as the latter alternative implies the final rejection of the Scriptures, the difficulties present themselves in this form. If Christ is not God, then the Scriptures afford no proof that there is a God at all, because the very proof to which the Deity himself appeals, is valid for the establishment of the Godhead of Christ; and if the peculiar proofs of the Divine existence are thus emasculated, there is no evidence for it in nature, as the Scriptures say. But this is seen to be absurd, hence the Scriptures must be cast away, together with their Author! Our proofs are the following:

1. Gen. 1 : 1.—In the *beginning* GOD CREATED the heavens and the earth.

John 1 : 1, 3.—In the *beginning* was the Word, and the Word was GOD—all things WERE MADE by him.

It can not be doubted that the Word of which John speaks, is Christ; for "the Word was made flesh and dwelt among us." Christ, then, by his testimony, was in the beginning, and made all things; but Moses says, that He who in the beginning created the heavens and earth is *God*, therefore Christ is *God*.

2. Ps. 102 : 25.—Of old hast THOU (Jehovah) laid the foundation of the earth: and the heavens are the work of thy hands.

Heb. 1 : 8, 10.—But unto the Son, he saith—THOU Lord, in the beginning hast laid the foundation of the earth; and the heavens are the works of thine hand.

The very words that David uses to describe the *works of God*, Paul borrows to describe the *works of Christ*. God himself appeals to his own works as the *proof* of His own Supreme Godhead; therefore, with reverence be it spoken, if the Divine argument be worth any thing, the same works must be appealed to in proof of the SUPREME GODHEAD OF CHRIST. If not, the argument can not prove the existence of God at all!

3. Jer. 10 : 10–12.—But JEHOVAH is the TRUE GOD, he is the LIVING GOD, and an EVERLASTING KING; at his wrath the earth shall tremble, and the nations shall not be able to endure his indignation. Thus shall ye say unto them. The gods that have not made the heavens and the earth, even they shall perish from the earth, and from under these heavens. He hath made the earth by his power, he hath established the world by his wisdom, and hath stretched out the heavens by his direction.

1 John 5 : 20. 1 Cor. 8 : 6. Rev. 19 : 16.—Christ is THE TRUE GOD AND ETERNAL LIFE, BY WHOM ARE ALL THINGS, THE KING OF KINGS AND LORD OF LORDS.

The first of these quotations pronounces a threatening upon those gods that men worship, whose nothingness shall be made manifest when they shall perish from the earth, from under heaven, by the hand of Him who made both, and whom both declare to be the Supreme God, Jehovah, the true God, and the everlasting King. The other three declare that He by whom all things are, is the true God, eternal Life and everlasting King. But this is the description of Christ; Christ is therefore proved by creation, to be the Supreme God.

4. Is. 44 : 24.—Thus saith JEHOVAH, thy Redeemer, and he that formed thee from the womb, I am JEHOVAH that maketh all things: that stretcheth forth the heavens ALONE, that spreadeth abroad the earth by MYSELF.

Col. 1 : 16, 17.—By him (Christ) were ALL THINGS CREATED, that are in heaven, and that are in earth, VISIBLE AND INVISIBLE, whether they be thrones or dominions, principalities or powers: all things were created by him and for him, and he is BEFORE all things, and by him all things CONSIST.

In the one passage, Jehovah is said to be the maker of *all things*, alone by himself. In the other Christ is said to be the maker of *all things* in heaven and earth—all that is visible in earth, all that is invisible in heaven, and by him all things consist; so that creation and providence are both ascribed to Christ. The 14th, 15th, and 16th verses of this chapter are parenthetically thrown in, to exhibit the Almighty power of our Redeemer, that the Colossians might have confidence in his supremacy, and see the folly of those seducers who sought to induce them to worship angels. Very pertinent, therefore, to his design was this magnificent description of our exalted Lord.

But what words can make it plainer that Christ is the Supreme God? The Apostle is really verbose in bringing this peculiar proof of Deity to bear upon our doctrine with all possible power. Not only the generality of things *visible,* but the totality of things *invisible* were made by Him. Paul seems also to guard us against supposing Christ to be a mere instrument; he tells us that he is *before* all things, and by him all things *consist;* which latter sentence proves the *preposition* to refer to *time*, and not to *dignity.* Paul says, *all things* were made by him, and John says *no one thing* was made without him, thus making him the God of providence as well as of creation. Now compare this with what the Prophet says: "Jehovah alone by himself made all things;" and conviction, it appears to us, must flash like lightning, blasting all doubt in the heart of every man who has ever had a doubt on this subject.

But if this be not satisfactory, what can be? If Christ be not God, he must be a creature: and then the monstrous absurdity follows, that *he made himself!* For if "without him *nothing* was made that was made," then surely this creature was his own Creator!! And if he could make, he can unmake himself at pleasure! More than this, *he can be and not be* at the same moment!!

Reason and Revelation unite in producing belief, that it is by his works, the being and attributes of God are proved. Without an appeal to these, we never could prove his existence. Now, if Christ be only a creature, we are utterly deprived of this source of proof, and of all others besides; because there is no work of God that is not performed by Him. Paul says he made all things, *visible* and *invisible*, but these embody every possible existence out of God. And if creation and providence prove the eternal power and Godhead of the Deity, must not the same works prove the eternal power and Godhead of Christ? They who deny the doctrine for which we contend are therefore reduced to this dilemma:

Either they must admit the Supreme GODHEAD OF CHRIST, *or say that God has no peculiar work by which he is distinguished from his creatures! They must admit that we have no proof that there is a God at all!!!* And this is BLANK ATHEISM.

We know that none who deny our doctrine, admit the conclusions which we assert, flow from their creed. It is for them to examine whether they are fairly drawn, and they are deeply interested; for if any hold a belief from which they necessarily flow as *consequences*, the question is, will not God hold them *responsible* for these consequences? Will not the general principle upon which God treats his creatures apply in their case, as in that of the Jews to whom Christ announced it: "If I had not come and spoken unto them, they had not had sin; but now they have no cloak for their sin." The *evidences* of the divinity of Christ, given in the sacred Scriptures, are as *strong* as the evidences for the divinity of God the Father; if not, we should

5

be glad to know in what respects the latter are stronger than the former. If men are condemned, as being "without excuse," for not believing *the thing* proved by the light of nature, in respect to *God*, will they not be held to a strict account, for not believing the *same thing* proved by the combined light of nature and of revelation in respect to *Christ?* "He that rejecteth me," says our Lord, "and recieveth not my words, hath one that judgeth him: the word that I have spoken, the same shall judge him at the last day." "He that believeth not God, hath made him a liar; because he believeth not *the record* that God gave of his Son. And this is the record, that God hath given to us eternal life, and this life is IN his Son." We really can see no difference between denying that Christ is THE ONLY LORD GOD, and "denying THE ONLY LORD GOD, and (even) OUR LORD JESUS CHRIST." (Jude 4th v.) They appear to us to be identically the same proposition, and if so, this denial must be the rejection of the record, the consequence of which is, "making God a liar"! And for this consequence of belief, or rather disbelief, men must answer.

CHAPTER VI.

V. DILEMMA: *Either Christ is God, or there is no peculiar worship by which God can be distinguished from his creatures.*

Quotation from Channing commented upon—Examples of Worship—Scripture Proofs—Consequence—Quotations from Priestley and Channing—Dilemma Verified.

BY Worship we mean *adoration*, the highest act of divine honor. They who esteem Christ as inferior to God allow that he is to be worshipped, but not in the sense of the duty we owe the Supreme Being. Dr. Channing, in attempting to reply to the objection, "that we read in the New Testament that Jesus was again and again worshipped, and that in admitting this he manifested himself to be the object of religious adoration," thus discourses: "It is wonderful that this fallacy, so often exposed, should be still repeated. Jesus indeed received worship or homage, but this was not offered as adoration to the infinite God; it was the homage which, according to the custom of the age and of the eastern world, was paid to men invested with great authority, whether in civil or religious concerns."

Mere *assertion* avails but little in exposing a fallacy, and we think that the *wonder* which excited the astonishment of the Doctor, will continue to the end of the world, if such be the way in which this fallacy is "so often exposed." To our comprehension, the *expose* is altogether on the other side. This alleged *fallacy*, is met with a confidence which always betrays the weakness of a bald assertion. Where any position is thus assailed, without presenting any thing better for an expose than a dashing *ipse dixit*, pitted against *high authority*, and *stubborn facts* glossed over by a general appeal to explanatory circumstances, the imbecility of the attack only exposes the strength of that position. With equal confidence do we say, that the "custom of the age," allowing it all the strength and influenc e that any custom may obtain, *can not* account for the language of the New Testament in reference to the worship due and paid our Lord Jesus Christ.

We have shown that all the *names* that are used to designate the object of supreme worship, are applied to Christ. We have shown that God can not *appear* in any form; and by the precision of Paul's language, that the *future* appearing of Christ will be the appearing of the *great God*, that is, the personality of the invisible God united with the visible Christ at his coming. Why, then, should we for a moment hesitate to render divine homage to our Redeemer?

When we turn to the Old Testament, we meet with the mention of numerous *appearances* of God.

Gen. 12 : 7, 8; 26 : 24, 25; 35 : 1–7.—And God said unto Jacob, Arise, go unto Bethel, and dwell there; and make there an *altar unto God that appeared unto thee*, etc.

Now, all are agreed that God the Father did not *appear* to the patriarchs and prophets. Who then did? Let a divinely-inspired expositor answer.

John 12 : 41.—These things said Esaias when he SAW *his glory* and spake of him," (CHRIST.) Compare Is. 6 : 3–5.

Christ then *appeared* under the Old Testament; but the direction given to Jacob was to make an altar unto God that *appeared;* and as John has shown that this was Christ spoken of by Isaiah, "Mine eyes have *seen* the King Jehovah of hosts," and as erecting altars was for the performance of the highest acts of divine worship, the matter would seem to be settled.

It was this glorious *appearance*, that filled the temple, and the Angel of the Covenant in whom was the name Jehovah, was enthroned upon the mercy-seat. "I will *appear* in the cloud on the mercy-seat." And to him was the prayer directed: "Give ear, O Shepherd of Israel, thou that leadest Joseph like a flock, thou that *dwellest between* the cherubim, shine forth."

Is. 40 : 10, 11.—Behold, the *Lord God* will come with strong hand, and his arm shall rule for him. Behold, *his reward is with him*, and his work before him. He shall feed his flock like a shepherd.

Rev. 22 : 12.—Behold, (said Christ,) I come quickly, and *my reward is with me.*

He who shall come with this reward to bestow upon his people, declared of himself thus:

John 10 : 11.—I am the good shepherd.

Christ was therefore the object of worship under the old economy. But when we peruse the gospel narrative, and the letters of instruction to the New-Testament Church, we find that Christ was worshipped from the first of his appearance as man on earth until his assumption into heaven.

When the Scriptures therefore represent the eastern Magi falling down and worshipping Christ; when they declare that those who were in the ship, at the time he caused Peter to walk on the water, worshipped him; when they tell us of a leper, of a ruler, of the Syro-Phœnician woman, of Mary Magdalene, of the other Mary, of his disciples, all worshipping him, without a single hint that this worship was not exactly *that* which he claimed as honor *equal* to the honor rendered to the Father, we must decline the belief that all this was nothing more than the observance of a prevalent custom of the east; we must believe it was something more than the expression of profound respect, or an exhibition of good manners: nay, considering the *extent* of Christ's claims, we must believe it to have been divine worship. Because Christ was *perfectly* good, we can come to no other conclusion; we can not suppose that a good man, even were he superior to angels, would allow such homage to be rendered to himself. When John, overcome by what he saw and heard, fell down to worship before the feet of the angel, (Rev. 22 : 8, 9,) he said: "See thou do it not; for I am thy fellow-servant;" but when others took the same attitude for the same purpose before Christ, he did not in like manner forbid it. However exalted as God's ambassador to our guilty world, if he were but a creature, Christ was a fellow-servant with other good men, and would have prevented such idolatry. He would have said: "See thou do it not —worship God."

Our position is demonstrated by the last act of Stephen, who was filled with the Holy Ghost, when he kneeled down and said: "Lord Jesus, receive my spirit." Was this prayer merely in conformity with an eastern custom by which Christ was wont to be honored, or was it an act of the highest worship? Let it be remarked that the *Man* Christ Jesus made the *same prayer* when he hung upon the cross. Now, if Stephen addressed to a creature the same prayer that creature addressed to the Creator, notwithstanding he was "full of the Holy Ghost," his last was the grossest act of idolatry.

Again. Just after the Ascension, the Apostle, together with a hundred and twenty disciples, *worshipped* Christ. "And they prayed and said, Thou, Lord, which knowest the hearts of all men, show whether of these two are chosen."

Paul, too, by example and by precept teaches us to *worship* Christ.

2 Cor. 12 : 8, 9.—For this thing I besought the Lord thrice that it might depart from me. And he said unto me, My grace is sufficient for thee; for my strength (power) is made perfect in weakness. Most gladly therefore will I rather glory in my infirmities, that the power of CHRIST may rest upon me.

1 Thessalonians 3 :11.—Now God himself, even our Father, and our Lord Jesus Christ direct our way unto you.

2 Thess. 2 : 16, 17.—Now our Lord Jesus Christ himself, and God even our Father, which hath loved us, and hath given us everlasting consolation and good hope through grace, comfort your hearts.

In the last two texts, prayer is addressed to God and Christ without respect to order of names, so that both are equally invoked.

Rom. 10 : 13.—Whosoever shall call upon the name of the Lord shall be saved.

The context shows that Christ is meant.

Rom. 14 :11, compared with Phil. 2 :10, 11.—"As I live, saith the Lord, *every knee* shall bow to me, and *every tongue shall confess* to God." "That at the name of Jesus *every knee* should bow, of things in heaven, and things in earth, and things under the earth; and that *every tongue* should confess that Jesus is Lord, to the glory of God the Father."

Phil. 2 : 19.—"I TRUST in the Lord Jesus to send Timotheus unto you."

Now, *trust*, as an act of dependence and pious devotion, is always spoken of in Scripture as the duty of men towards God *alone*. "Cursed is he that trusteth in man, and maketh flesh his arm." If then Christ be but a man, by trusting in him Paul fell under the execration of God.

Baptism is certainly an act of the highest religious

worship. Ministers are commanded to "baptize in the name of the Father, Son, and Holy Ghost;" but if the Son be a *creature*, and the Spirit an *influence*, what an absurdity follows?

Calling on the name of Jesus, is a phrase used to designate Christians as the worshippers of Christ.

1 Cor. 1 : 2.—Paul salutes "all that in *every place* call upon the name of Jesus Christ our Lord," that is, all who INVOKE Him.

Acts 9 : 14.—Here he hath authority from the chief-priests to bind all that call upon, or invoke thy name.

Rev. 5 : 8, 14.—John in Patmos had the glorious sight of "the four beasts, (creatures,) and four and twenty elders falling down before the *Lamb*, having every one of them harps, and golden vials full of odors which are *the prayers of the saints*."

"And I beheld, and I heard the voice of many angels round about the throne, and the beasts and the elders: and the number of them was ten thousand times ten thousand, and thousands of thousands; saying, with a loud voice, Worthy is the *Lamb* that was slain to receive power, and riches, and wisdom, and strength, and honor, and glory, and blessing. And every creature which is in heaven, and on the earth, and under the earth, and such as are in the sea, and all that are in them, heard I saying, Blessing, and honor, and glory, and power, be unto Him that sitteth upon the throne, and unto the Lamb for ever. And the four beasts said Amen. And the four and twenty elders fell down and worshipped Him that liveth for ever and ever."

Comment here is useless. If Christ, the Lamb, do not receive the highest act of divine homage, then it is impossible to tell what that homage is.

Again. God *commands* the worship of his Son.

Heb. 1 : 6.—And again, when he bringeth in the first begotten into the world, he saith, And let all the angels of God worship him.

If all angels, then surely all men must worship our glorious Redeemer.

Here, then, we have numerous examples and express declarations, sufficiently clear. Angels, apostles, martyrs, and all the redeemed render Him divine homage. But if Christ be not the Supreme God, then the horrid conclusion is inevitable, that the writers of the Bible have conspired to lead men into that sin which shall exclude them from heaven! A still more blasphemous consequence follows: *God himself has adopted every expedient to lead his creatures into that abominable sin which he hates!!* How can we escape this revolting consequence? Every *inducement* is offered us. The *most glorious names, attributes, works, and worship* are ascribed to Him; and upon the supposition that our Maker means to have us regard him as the Supreme God, no arguments more effective could possibly be presented. There is, therefore, no possibility of reconciling the two systems of faith which differ so widely on this subject; they are as opposite as light and darkness.

Hence Dr. Priestley says: "I do not wonder that you Calvinists entertain and express a strongly unfavorable opinion of us Unitarians. *The truth is*, there neither can, nor ought to be, any compromise between us. If *you* are right, WE ARE NOT CHRISTIANS AT ALL; and if *we* are right, YOU ARE GROSS

IDOLATERS." And Dr. Channing says: "That Jesus Christ, if exalted into the Infinite Divinity, should be more interesting than the Father, is precisely what might be expected from history, and from the principles of human nature. en want an object of worship like themselves, and the great secret of IDOLATRY lies in this propensity." Although the last quotation gives a very unfair turn to what the author knew to be the faith of his opponents, it serves to show that, like the former, he regarded the system based upon the Supreme Godhead of Christ, at perfect war with that which is mainly characterized by the denial of this VITAL POINT.

We like this outspoken honesty, but we deplore the faith in whose behalf it is enlisted. Their appeal is to *Reason;* so is ours; and as we think that we have proved our point from Scripture, reasonably interpreted, we have no hesitancy in saying, consisttency demands that they who deny our faith be reduced to this dilemma:

Either they must deny that the Supreme God has any peculiar worship by which he can be distinguished from his creatures, or they must admit that Christ is the Supreme God.

CHAPTER VII.

VI. DILEMMA: *Either Christ is the Supreme God, if he was, when on earth, a good man; or if he was only a man, only a creature, he must have been a very bad man.*

Quotations from Dr. Channing and the Koran—Christ understood his own Nature—His Trials—Christ before the Sanhedrim—Their conduct—Christ put under Oath—His Condemnation—Meaning of the phrase, "Son of God"—How the Jews understood it—The Character he had acquired—He confirmed them in their Interpretation of his Words—Consequences—Can not get rid of them—Another Court Session—Their Civil Accusation—Christ before Pilate—His Honesty in Explanation—His Acquittal—Pilate's infamous Conduct—Consequences—Dilemma verified.

THE honor and glory of our blessed Redeemer are dear to us. It is indeed revolting and heart-sickening to dwell upon the terrible consequences that seem to flow from the denial of his Divinity, yet we believe a plain statement of these must have more weight with readers in general, than all the critical display that the profoundest philogist can make.

Some maintain that our Saviour preëxisted before he came in the flesh, that he is the most glorious creature of God, and appeared in human form. But this opinion can not rationally be entertained for a moment, because it denies the human nature of

Christ; it substitutes a glorious spiritual existence in the place of the *human soul* of our Redeemer, and invests him merely with the shell of our humanity. But the most of those who are opposed to the doctrine we contend for, maintain that he was nothing more nor less than a perfectly good man, around whose character cluster all the fascinations of unequalled virtue.

With both of these views we think the Scriptures wholly irreconcilable. Dr. Channing says, (vol. 4: 168:) "You will easily understand what I esteem the ground of love to Christ. It is his spotless purity, his moral perfection, and his unsullied goodness." "I can direct you to nothing in Christ more important than his tried and victorious and perfect goodness. Others may love Christ for mysterious attributes. I love him for the rectitude of his soul and life." "I love him, I have said, for his moral excellence: I know nothing else." The Koran speaks in terms equally honorable to our Saviour: "O Mary! verily God sendeth thee good tidings, thou shalt hear the word proceeding from himself: his name shall be CHRIST JESUS, the son of Mary, honorable in this world and in the world to come, and one of those who approach near to the presence of God; and he shall speak unto men in the cradle, and when he is grown up; and he shall be one of the righteous."

Now, on the supposition that Christ was only a man, such compliments may seem very pretty, but we think them unmerited and absurd; compliments both ill-judged and misplaced simply for this reason, that he was in reality a *bad* man. This is a painful statement; our pen falters, and nothing but an earnest desire to convince men of the falsity of the system that aims to pluck the diadem from the King of kings and Lord of lords, our Divine Redeemer, prompts us to go on.

All who acknowledge the Bible to have come from God, believe in the divine origin of Christianity, and think their faith corroborated from its history in the moral renovation of men and nations. This religion teaches us that Jesus Christ came to establish it upon the ruins of false systems, and soul-destroying delusions. From the time its glorious Founder left the world, it has made progress, has been perpetuated, and is preserved by means wholly unknown in the history of any other religion. As it was novel, so it was seemingly inadequate to realize the expectations of its early adherents; yet four centuries only had elapsed, when it was established upon the throne of the Cæsars. It has accomplished a revolution in the world that has secured the most valuable benefits to its population, and its successes already gained, are sure pledges that its final results will be in accordance with the doctrines and predictions of Jesus. These must convince us that he perfectly understood his own nature, offices, and works. To admit the divine origin of his religion and that he came from God, is to admit that he was wholly incapable of deceiving or being deceived, and that on no occasion could he either designedly or undesignedly make false impressions, much less publish false facts for deception, or the accomplishment of his purposes.

This admitted, the whole of the inquiry as to his divinity is narrowed down to the meaning of the simple declarations he made of himself, when under a formal process of trial before the Jewish Sanhedrim, and in Pilate's court. Let us, then, review in their mutual bearing, for the sake of the best of evidence,

CHRIST'S TRIALS.

Respecting this interesting portion of our Saviour's history, many do not see the main points of the plot, owing perhaps partly to the brevity of each of the historians, who wrote according to the respective impressions the facts in the case made upon their minds; and partly to their own method of reading the sacred narrative in detached portions. A little attention to collating the four accounts which the Evangelists give of the last hours of our Lord's eventful life, will serve to present the whole in satisfactory view. When we compare these, we find that He was tried before two tribunals, on two separate and distinct charges. The one was the Jewish Sanhedrim, where he was tried on the charge of BLASPHEMY, and *condemned;* the other was the Roman Governor's court, where he was tried for the crime of HIGH TREASON, and *acquitted.* Let us look at the parties in both these trials.

I. Christ before the Sanhedrim.

"The time at which courts were held among the Jews, and causes were brought before them for trial was in the morning. According to the Talmudists, it was not lawful to try causes of a capital nature in the night, and it was equally unlawful to examine a cause, pass sentence, and put it in execution the same day. This last particular was very strenuously insisted upon. It is worthy of remark, that all of these practices, which were observed in other trials, were neglected in the tumultuous trial of Jesus."*

By a stratagem to which the principal men of this court were a party, our Lord was taken and brought for trial before it in the night. It was hurriedly assembled at the house of the High-Priest. Thither Christ was taken by a lawless midnight rabble, with torches, staves, and clubs, whose conduct can be more easily conceived than described. In a summary way, this mockery of a trial was got up, and the High-Priest, who was the president of the court, "asked Jesus of his disciples, and of his doctrine." Jesus thus answered him: "I spake openly to the world: I ever taught in the synagogue, and in the temple, whither the Jews always resort, and in secret have I said nothing. Why askest thou me? ask them which heard me, what I have said unto them: behold, they know what I said."—Here was our Saviour manacled in the night, and arraigned

* Jahn's Archæology.

contrary to the law which prescribed the time and way of trial for the worst of criminals. But he did not complain, he openly and honestly answered the High-Priest, respectfully referring to those who knew him best, and by his answer he foiled them. Bound as he was, he had a double claim to protection from insult, yet an *officer* of this court, a heartless wretch, struck him a blow unrebuked. False witnesses then appeared to swear his life away, but their contradictory evidence promised ill-success. Now that these malicious bargainers for his blood had him in their power, they determined that they should not be disappointed.

Mortified at failure by the clashing of their own evidence, they thought to make him convict himself; and contrary to all righteousness and law, withholding that magnanimity, to which a helpless criminal is by his very position entitled, they did their best to lead him into an altercation, in hopes of perverting his words to his own destruction. But Christ "opened not his mouth." He calmly listened to the disgraceful proceedings of this bitterly grave tribunal, without saying a word. Pretending that their dignity was highly insulted by his silence, the High-Priest made a direct assault upon him for not putting in a *plea* against a charge which, upon the testimony offered, ought to have been instantly quashed; buts till he held his peace, until it was manifest their efforts were abortive.

As a last resort, enraged at failure, the High-

Priest said: "I adjure thee, by the living God, that thou tell us whether thou be the Christ, the Son of God." In capital cases it was lawful to swear the person accused. God had ordained, that when it was difficult to come at the truth, "an oath of the Lord," should be administered to the party accused; and the greatest guilt rested upon him who in such circumstances, did not unequivocally tell the truth. (Ex. 22 : 11, Lev. 5 : 1.) Therefore, Jesus calmly replied: "Thou hast said; nevertheless, I say unto you, hereafter shall ye see the Son of Man sitting on the right hand of power, and coming in the clouds of heaven." Then the High-Priest, pretending to be horror-stricken, rent his clothes and said: "He hath spoken *blasphemy*, what further need have we of witness? behold, now ye have heard his *blasphemy*. What think ye? They answered and said, He is guilty of death." And they spit in his face, and struck him with violence!!

This is the whole offense, and these last, are the words upon which he was sentenced, according to the law. (Lev. 24 : 16.) The question demanded whether Jesus was the *Messiah — the Son of God*. The answer affirmed that he was both the *Son of God*, and the *Son of man*, and the final Judge! It is doubtful whether the Jews, in the time of Christ, believed that their Messiah was to be Divine. That their fathers thought so, appears from the Targums, and the question was put in such a way that the answer should be explicit on this *point*. And Christ was explicit. He asserted that he was the Son of man, that is, literally man; and that he was the Son of God, that is, literally God, as they understood it; and that he would be the Judge of the world. That he was the Son of man, no one disputed; but the blasphemy consisted in the phrase, *Son of God.* To put his meaning beyond a doubt, he added, that he would be the final Judge.

Now, the phrase, Son of God, is susceptible of three meanings, namely: simple origin, general likeness, and identity of nature. In which of these did he use it? It clearly could not have been in the sense of simple origin, for the last prophet said: "Have we not all one Father, hath not one God created us?" Nor could it have been in the sense of general likeness, since Adam was called a son of God, and magistrates also. These uses of this phrase were well known, and it would have been infinitely absurd in the Jewish Court, to have pronounced the expression blasphemous in either of these significations. They therefore must have understood him to mean, identity of nature; and in this sense, for a man to call himself the Son of God, would, of course, be gross blasphemy. As Christ, therefore, could only be a blasphemer in this last sense, and as by the *additional* explanatory words, he confirmed them in the belief that he claimed *identity of nature with God*, it is perfectly evident that he meant to assert his own Supreme Godhead.

Whenever there is any dispute about a phrase,

our shortest and best method is, to find out what they understand by it, to whom it is addressed. This charge of blasphemy, was not now made for the first time against Christ; it had been frequently brought in his controversies with the Jews. On one occasion he said: "I and my Father are one." The question respecting this assertion, is not what it really means, or what it may be made to mean, but what was the *impression* it made upon the hearers, what idea did it convey to them? Their indignation, we find, was so aroused, that they "took up stones to stone him." Now, Christ well knew what was meant by this action; for the blasphemer, by the Mosaic law, was to be *stoned;* yet he inquired the reason. "Because," said they, mark the answer, "Because thou being a *man*, makest thyself *God.*" Did Christ correct them? He did not. He confirmed them in their interpretation of his words. (John 5 : 18.) "The Jews sought the more to kill him, because he had not only broken the Sabbath, but said also that God was his (own, ἴδιον) Father, *making himself equal with God.*" Did he deny this? See v. 23: "All men should honor the Son, *even as* they honor the Father. He that honoreth not the Son honoreth not the Father which hath sent him." Now, these last words are not exegetical of the former sentence, for no *Messenger* is ever honored in the manner that the *Sender* is honored. If they had *misunderstood* him, would not common honesty, as well as common prudence, and common piety, have led him to correct the mistake? Doubtless. But he did not do it. He left upon their minds the burning impression, that he claimed to be the ETERNAL GOD. He was virtually invited to remove it. It was distinctly announced to him, that he should be stoned for a blasphemous claim which he, a *man*, had the audacity and the impiety to make.

Now, were he only a man, is it possible to consider him in any degree a *good* man? How can we escape the conclusion that all his apparent goodness was only successful artifice by which he sought to elevate himself to the rank of those deified heroes that were worshipped by the blind devotees of Greece and Rome?

On another occasion, he appropriated to himself the peculiar name of Jehovah—I AM; and they attempted to stone him, but instead of waiting to explain, he escaped.

Again. At another time, he brought them into confusion by a dilemma. "The Pharisees had heard that he had put to silence the Sadducees," and they thought they would try their wits upon him; but, to their surprise, in a very summary way, he thus brought them to their wits' end. "What think ye of Christ? whose son is he? They say unto him the Son of David. He saith unto them: How then doth David in spirit call him LORD? saying, The LORD said unto my LORD, Sit thou on my right hand, till I make thine enemies thy footstool. If David then called him LORD, how is he his Son?

And no man was able to answer him a word." The Psalm referred to is the 110th, where Jehovah is represented as saying to him whom David calls LORD, "Be thou (σὺνθρονος) with me—a partner of my throne." Now, if Christ is the Son of David, "How then," said Jesus, "doth David call him Lord?—If David called him Lord, how is he his Son?" Among the Hebrews, children were never entitled to, and could not claim such deference from a parent of more exalted rank. This was well understood; therefore the question was confounding. They had not a word to say. They were not half so cunning as Dr. Channing. What a pity they did not think of his solution. "It was the homage which according to the age was paid to men invested with great authority"!* They knew that he claimed to be the Messiah. On the supposition that the Messiah is divine, the question is easily answered; but if he be a *mere man*, as the *Pharisees* held, it is impossible to solve it. They saw his drift, they knew his meaning, and were enraged the more, because they could not successfully meet him.

From these instances it is perfectly plain, that Christ had actually acquired the character of a bold blasphemer among the Jews, long before his arrest. And when arrested, UNDER OATH he confirmed the impression that he "made himself God" by declaring, not only that he was the *Son of man*, but the *Son of God*, and also the *final Judge*. His condemnation

* Channing's Works, v. 4, p. 315.

was therefore pronounced, on the ground that he was guilty of blasphemy, and sought to lead the people to pay divine homage to himself. No candid man, it appears to us, can resist the conclusion that they understood the expression "Son of God," in the last sense we have mentioned, namely, *identity of nature.* Nor can it be doubted that Christ was fully aware they thus understood him: and that they understood him rightly, is evident from the fact, that Jesus, who on all *other* occasions was quick to point out their mistakes, did not say that they apprehended him in a wrong sense. He did not upbraid them with putting any forced construction upon his words. As none knew better than he, the meaning of language, and as "He knew what was in man, and needed not that any should teach him," he designedly used an expression to denote his own Supreme Godhead, which the Jewish Court, in view of his already acquired character, and in view of all the circumstantial details of his controversies with the Jews on this very point, could not misunderstand. How could they? His assertions were plain. No equivocation, no explanation, no apology escaped him, but he meant to make the impression he did make. They knew what he said, and he knew what they understood. There was, therefore, no mistake.

Now, if Christ thus affirming, and thus well understood, be not truly and properly God, *coëqual* with the Father, it follows that the Jews were *right* when they denounced him as a "wretch not fit to live," for he bore false witness against himself, and thus was a *perjured* man! In consequence of this, his blood was upon his own head; because, in virtue of his own testimony he was condemned, when a simple declaration of the *truth* might have saved his life: therefore he was in fact a *suicide!* Inasmuch as he refused to disabuse the court of wrong impressions which he himself had made and confirmed, and must have known it, he was *superlatively dishonest!* Because he set himself up as an IDOL, and is the author of the most stupendous system of idolatry the world ever saw, the most righteous act the Jewish court ever did, was to *condemn* him!

We do not see how it is possible to get rid of these horrid consequences which make us tremble as we write. Deny his Divinity, and you must say, that when Christianity was triumphant, various forms of idolatry gave way, only to make room for another more *monstrous* than either, or all of them put together; and we poor deluded idolaters, are spending our exertions and exhausting our zeal, to convert certain other poor deluded idolaters to a system of error, more fraught with death than their own!! Deny his Divinity, and you brand him at once with infamy, provided these conclusions are fairly drawn. How any, in view of his failure to disabuse the court of wrong impressions, when such tremendous consequences follow, how any can regard him either as *good, moral, or virtuous,* is beyond our ken.

It is clearly a quibble to say, that our Lord was not *obliged* to explain the phraseology he used, by which he had acquired a character so detestable in the eyes of his nation; it is the very poorest evasion to say, he was not *obliged* to explain before the Jewish court, nor to correct any of their misconceptions; for who does not see that in point of veracity, a man betrays the very worst moral obliquity, when he uses *designedly* an expression in *one* sense, and knows, at the same time, that they to whom it is addressed, must understand it in *another?* Would not this conduct reflect upon our Saviour just as much as the most palpable falsehood? Certainly. He who is truth itself, never could have acted thus. This is proved by his demeanor before Pilate on his second trial, where he was as honest in preventing misconceptions of the truth, as he had before been candid in enforcing its claims.

After the disgraceful proceedings of the night, when the Sanhedrim passed sentence of death upon our Lord, and maltreated him in the most brutal manner, they thought it expedient to have another meeting. Accordingly, "very early in the morning, all the chief-priests and elders of the people with the scribes and the whole council, held an assembly to consult *how* they might put Jesus to death." They had condemned him, but it was a question whether they could secure his execution; for the Romans had taken away from them the power to inflict capital punishment. It was necessary, therefore, to have him condemned by the Roman power, if they would have him executed by Roman authority, and by Roman means of punishment.

The expedient they next hit upon was, to accuse Christ of HIGH TREASON. The Romans very well knew what was their expectation, in reference to the Messiah, and that the time had elapsed by their calculation, for the appearance of a great military chieftain who should free them from their vassalage to that empire. That great solicitude was felt on this subject, is evident from the horrid act of Herod, by whose bloody decree the babes of Bethlehem were slain, in hopes of cutting off their expected Messiah. It was very natural, therefore, that this assembly should think it an admirable plan to take advantage of this feeling of jealousy on the part of the government; for they rightly judged that any one advancing the claims of a king, as Christ had done, would stand a poor chance of escape. To make sure of better testimony than that of the unlucky blunderers whom they had suborned, they led Christ into their council a second time, black with bruises, and disfigured by barbarous violence. Although he had been condemned, they determined to put him upon another, and a more public trial; and they began by going over the same ground, with the view, however, of mainly pressing him upon his claim of being the Messiah. "Art thou the Messiah? Tell us. And he said unto them: If I tell you, ye will not believe; and if I also interrogate you, ye will not answer me, nor let me go. Hereafter shall the *Son of man* sit on the right hand of the power of God. Then said they all, Art thou *the Son of God?* and he said unto them, I am. And they said, What need we any further witness? for we ourselves have heard of his own mouth."

They now had again a full confession that he claimed to be both *God* and *man*, and by consequence the *Messiah*. "And the whole multitude of them led him away to Pilate."

II. Christ before Pilate.

It was important for the Sanhedrim to obtain the death of Christ if they could, on the sentence of their *own* court, to sustain their reputation with the people; for the very fact of their being obliged to go to the Roman governor in this matter, reminded them of their abject existence as a nation. Arrived at the door of the Prætorium, for fear of contracting defilement from Gentiles, these sanctimonious hypocrites would not go in. Pilate, aware of their scruples, came out into the paved court, and seeing a prisoner bound, said to them: "What accusation bring ye against this man?" By this, their dignity was much affronted, as if it were an insult to suspect them of asking the death of an innocent man; and they replied: "If he were not a malefactor, we would not have delivered him up unto thee." Pilate knew their character too well to be deceived by their pretensions, and as they made no accusation, he gave them to understand that if *they* had so adjudged, so they might deal with him according to their law. This was bitter irony, and they had to state the reason why they came to him: "It is not lawful for us to put any man to death." Pilate having insisted upon an indictment, and knowing that the Roman law would not regard the penalties of the Jewish, they concluded to prefer against him the crime of HIGH TREASON. "We found this fellow perverting the nation, and forbidding to give tribute to Cæsar, saying that he himself is Christ, (the Messiah,) a King."

This ground apparently was the most promising that could be taken, for should he deny that he ever proclaimed himself a King, there would be an end to his career, as he would have been branded by a hundred oaths with palpable falsehood; and if, on the other hand, he should make the assertion that he was a *King*, it must be taken as a plea of guilt: so they thought themselves sure of their suit.

Here, then, was some need of explanation upon the part of Christ; for although the naked assertion, that he was a King, was true, in Pilate's court it would have conveyed a false impression. Did our Saviour either refuse to explain or deny his claims? He did not. He plainly did the one, and boldly maintained the other. "Then Pilate called Jesus, and said unto him, Art thou the king of the Jews? And he answering, said unto him, Thou sayest." Now if he had stopped here, a false impression might have procured his condemnation. Truth demanded that Pilate should know the *exact* sense in which he used that word. Therefore our Lord informed him: "My kingdom is not of this world: if my kingdom were of this world, then would my servants fight, that I should not be delivered to the Jews: but now is my kingdom not from hence." This at once served to quiet the apprehensions of the governor, if he had any; but he proceeded to reïterate the question, and Christ varied his explanation. "Art thou a king then?" "Thou sayest that I am a king. To this end was I born, and for this cause came I into the world, that I should bear witness unto the truth. Every one that is of the truth, heareth my voice." Pilate was satisfied with the explanation. He saw clearly that Christ laid no claim to temporal power, to the prejudice of the Roman Government; and since he had no ambition for the royal purple, he was convinced he harbored no treasonable designs against his monarch. Then Pilate went out to the Jews, who were waiting the issue in anxious expectation of the condemnation of Christ, and announced his ACQUITTAL.

After Pilate had made repeated attempts to release him, exasperated beyond measure, they clamored for the worst of punishments, and said: "We have a law, and by our law he ought to die, *because he made himself the* SON OF GOD." Can any man fail to see they interpreted this phrase in the sense of *identity of nature* with God? Did they not say so? and did not Christ know that such was their understanding? Beyond a doubt, he knew it. Could he not have easily met and vanquished them on this point, in Pilate's court, had they misinterpreted his words, or misunderstood his meaning? Inasmuch as Pilate had acquitted him before them all, could he not have shown that their law did not reach him at all, by simply exposing their mistake, had they made one? Under the circumstances, and in view of the consequences, let any good man ask himself what he would have done, and what Christ ought to have done, had he been placed in a false position before the Roman court. We think no man of common-sense can help seeing, that if Christ was a good man, he could not have allowed his enemies to misrepresent his claims, when he was in a court not under their sway; that if he were God as well as man, there is consistency in his conduct; that if he were not God, there was not only inconsistency, but great wickedness shown by him, to his utter disgrace as a man of truth.

We need not enlarge upon the way in which this unjust judge was intimidated by the disappointed and furious mob. Since Pilate had acquitted him of the crime they brought, they insanely called upon him to execute the sentence of their court; threatening him, if he did not, with an accusation before Cæsar for disloyalty and breach of trust, in refusing to punish a criminal condemned by his own nation, and accused of high treason. "If thou let this man go, thou art not Cæsar's friend. Whosoever maketh himself a king, speaketh against Cæsar." His cowardice prompted him to act in direct violation of his own convictions, for "he knew that the chief-priests had delivered him for envy;" yet for the sake of policy, and dreading the execution of their threat, regardless of the life of an innocent man, deaf to the remonstrance of conscience, he yielded to their will. Thus, Christ died a martyr to the doctrine of his own SUPREME GODHEAD.

No candid man will say, that our Lord was not equally honest before the Jewish tribunal and the Roman court. In the former, he was understood to assert his own proper divinity, and was adjudged guilty of blasphemy, "because being a man, he made himself God." This was the exposition all along put upon his words, and on this account he had acquired the character of a blasphemer, and finally was condemned for blasphemy; and by a strange combination of circumstances, for this sin against the Jewish law, he was made to suffer a Roman punishment. Now, if he were not God, but only a very good man, why did he not *explain*, as he did before Pilate? Why did he not reject with disdain an imputation so foul, that *failure to disavow. ought for ever to extinguish the pretensions of the best man that ever lived?* Here is a corner from which there is no getting out. If Christ were really a good man, he must also be God; but if he be not God, if he be but a creature, then to us the consequence seems inevitable, he must have been the *very worst of bad men!* a deceiver, a perjured man, a suicide, and a fool for dying in support of a false fact!! His disciples are idolaters! every Christian misled by the Bible to believe in his divinity, is divinely misled; and the most pious are the most impious; and their cherished system of religion, the worst that ever cursed the world!! Thus, the opposers of our doctrine must meet another dilemma, if they would be consistent, as "rational Christians" ought to be:

Either they must admit that Christ, if only a man, was A VERY BAD MAN, *or if a good man, that he is the* SUPREME GOD.

CHAPTER VIII.

VII. DILEMMA.—*Either Christ is God, or he is not the Messiah.* His Offices proved—Divinity of the Messiah—What the Messiah was to do—Consequences if he be not Divine—Dilemma verified—An inconsistency.

THE word *Messiah* means the "anointed." It was a custom among the Hebrews to anoint with oil their High-Priests, (Ex. 30 : 25–30,) and their Prophets and Kings. (1 Kings 19 : 16.) The Prophets proclaimed the appearance of a *great Prophet*, an *everlasting Priest*, and a *glorious King*, who, combining these three offices in himself, was *anointed* by God to execute all their duties in teaching, redeeming, and reigning over his own chosen people. (Is. 45 : 7; 61 : 1; Dan. 9 : 24, 25, 26.) "Messiah the Prince," thus foretold in the Old Testament, is CHRIST, or the "anointed" of the New. He is called "the Prophet of the highest." (Luke 1 : 76.) "The High-Priest of our profession," (Heb. 3 : 1,) and "King of kings." (Rev. 19 : 16.)

By proving the divinity of Christ, we of course prove the divinity of the Messiah.—That He was expected to be a divine person is abundantly evident from the Scriptures, and from writings of the ancient Hebrews; though it is with great probability supposed, that in the time of our Saviour the Jews lost the faith of their fathers, and believed their Messiah was to be but a man, raised up to restore their nation to superior greatness and renown. With their belief so secularized and perverted, we have nothing to do. We simply and briefly will show that if Christ be not God, he was not the Messiah.

The Messiah is a proper name applied to the expected Deliverer, whose advent into the world, for ages past, has been the hope and consolation of Israel. The nature and work descriptive of him in the Old Testament, when ascertained, will show us what Christ is, if he be the Messiah. Here we shall be as brief as possible, inasmuch as the reader, by recurring to passages already quoted, can easily make his own comment.

I. As to his nature—he was to be a *Man.* As all are agreed on this matter, we need not quote the various offices he should discharge, all implying his strict and proper manhood. But he is more than man. How much more, must be ascertained from the declarations of the Old Testament.

The 45th Psalm was always understood by the Jews to refer to their Messiah. In the 6th v. the king spoken of is called *God.* Its application to Christ, by Paul, in Heb. 1, is beyond question. The Messiah is called a *Branch of Jehovah,* (Is. 4 : 2; comp. Is. 11 : 1; Zech. 3 : 8; 6 : 12.) *Jehovah our righteousness*, is the name of this Branch. (Jer. 23 : 5, 6; Jer. 33 : 16.) "This is he who shall call to her, Jehovah our Righteousness."

The Messiah is called by name, Wonderful, Counsellor, The Mighty God, The Everlasting Father, The Prince of Peace. (Is. 9 : 6, 7.)

The Messiah is called *Jehovah, God.* (Is. 40 : 3–5, 9–11.)

The One known as the Angel of Jehovah, and the Angel of the Covenant, under the Patriarchal and Mosaic dispensations, was their future Messiah. Rabbinical authors frequently refer these names to him; but the appellations, attributes, and worship of the Deity are given to this august person, and acts of distinct personality are ascribed to the Angel of Jehovah. He is represented as the proper object of assured confidence and of religious worship; therefore he was to be *God* as well as man.

Now, all Christians admit that Christ is the Messiah; but if Unitarianism be true, he can not be that Deliverer, because he is not entitled to the appellatives and the honors ascribed to the Messiah in the Old Testament.

II. As to his work, it is said:

Is. 2 : 18.—*And the* IDOLS *he shall utterly abolish.*

The chapter containing this prediction, speaks of what was to happen in the last days: "Out of Zion shall go forth the law, and the word of the Lord from Jerusalem" This was signally fulfilled when the Messiah commissioned his Apostles to preach the gospel to every creature. The Messiah, then, is to abolish idols utterly; but if Christ be not God, he is not Messiah, for he has done nothing towards abolishing idolatry. So far from this, he has been exalted as the greatest and most dangerous of all idols, Christians have been and are the grossest idolaters, and Christianity is the worst system of idolatry that has ever appeared!

The Koran says: "The *temptation* to idolatry is more grievous than to kill in the sacred months." "Where are the idols which ye called upon besides God?—God shall say unto them at the resurrection, Enter ye with the nations which have preceded you, of genii and of men, into hell-fire." Mohammedanism is therefore a better system than Christianity, which exalts a *man* into an idol! Mohammed is better than Christ, who receives divine homage as God, when he is but a man; and the prophet of Mecca has better claims to the Messiahship than Jesus of Nazareth, because he succeeded better in abolishing idols! And the *Koran* is better than the *Bible*, which is full of *temptation* to idolatry!! Consistency, then, would seem to demand, that they who deny the divinity of our Saviour, should *prefer* Mohammedanism to Christianity.

If Christ be only a creature, for eighteen hundred years he has been the object of idolatrous worship, and all the idols his system of religion ever abolished, simply yielded their place to another and a worse idol in his own person. Therefore, consistency demands that the opponents of our doctrine should choose one of these alternatives:

Either they must admit that Christ is God, or deny that he is the Messiah.

So long as they call the worshippers of three Gods "fellow-Christians," and "brethren," they acknowledge *their* system to be *Christianity;* but nothing can be plainer than this, the same system can not teach Theism and Tritheism. There is no difference between a Tritheist and a Polytheist. We can not be Christians and Idolaters too. We therefore prefer from our opponents the *name* which precisely delineates our religious belief, as they think, to the heartless compliment which says one thing and means another.

CHAPTER IX.

OBJECTIONS FROM SCRIPTURE AND REASON ANSWERED.

The value of objections—Shifting ground—The fallacy of objections—Why we can not accept Unitarian faith—Our arguments not yet answered—Unitarian ratiocination—Our position not touched—Their proof-texts harmonize with our view—"Son of God" a title in harmony with our view of his nature—Quotations from Dr. Channing—Shown to be futile—Quotation from Dr. Dick—Dr. Channing's rule of exegesis—Its operation—Other vital doctrines denied—Personal salvation put in jeopardy.

IT becomes us to notice the principal objections which have been made to the doctrine advocated in these pages. We believe that men may be just as sincere in an error as in the truth, but *sincerity* can not blot out the eternal distinction between them, nor annul the differences they make in human character. Were it otherwise the mission of our Saviour would have been in vain; and the only conceivable preference of truth to error would be in the advantages that might accrue to the structure of human society; one system being the better, because the more favorable to the enjoyment of a greater amount of social happiness. Were it otherwise, the Hindoo would receive nothing better from Christianity as a religious system than emancipation from one routine of ceremonies to embrace another, or none at all, as might best suit him. Sincerity, however, is to be respected, while indifference is to be condemned. The objections to the former are entitled to consideration, the heartlessness of the latter can only claim pity, while it deserves contempt.

The only question which concerns us is this: Is the doctrine of Christ's Supreme Godhead fairly *proved* from Scripture, and from the *absurdities* that seem to to follow its denial, upon the supposition that the Bible is the inspired word of God? If so, objections can not destroy that proof. "Objections," says an ingenious writer, "against a thing fairly proved, are of no weight. The proof rests upon our knowledge, and the objections upon our ignorance. It is true that moral demonstrations, and religious doctrines may be attacked in a very ingenious and plausible manner, because they involve questions on which our ignorance is greater than our knowledge: but still our knowledge is knowledge; or, in other words, our certainty is certainty. When you have proved that the three angles of any triangle are equal to two right angles, there is an end of doubt; because there are no materials for ignorance to work up into phantoms." But there is a wider field for gathering such materials in moral and religious subjects, and their use is just to bring up such phantoms as shall delude us by their unsubstantial forms.

Now, in regard to the objections made to our doctrine from Scripture, they involve what is technically called "*ignoratio elenchi*," a mistake of the question, and the fallacy of *shifting ground*. The question is this: Is Christ the Supreme God? The argument brought to prove that he is *man*, shifts ground, because it does not maintain the *negative* of the real question; it only proves another proposition about which there is no dispute. We are all agreed that Christ is really and truly man; therefore, to bring proofs for this, instead of answering the proofs of the *affirmative* of the real question, is utterly irrelevant and evasive, for the conclusion that "Christ is not God," by no means follows.

We maintain it is egregious trifling to manage the controversy by imposing sophisms upon our readers, and certainly not creditable to "rational Christianity." Take the case of an astronomer, who proves the sun to be an opaque body. Surely his position can not be controverted, by showing that the sun is the source of light to our world. The *affirmative* of any proposition is not to be answered by supporting the *affirmative* of a different proposition. We complain therefore of our opponents that when we prove Christ to be *God*, they meet us by proving that he is *man*, about which there is no dispute. Why do they not meet the *only* question between us on the subject of his nature?

The "fallacy of objections" is this: "Showing that *there are* objections against some plan, theory, or system, and thence inferring that it should be rejected;

when that which ought to have been proved is, that there are *more* or *stronger* objections against the receiving than the rejecting of it." *Jesus Christ is the Supreme God.* Our objections to *rejecting* this as the truth, have been informally stated; but for the sake of contrasting their relative strength with that of those presented in opposition, we may be allowed to show them in a formal order.

1st. *All* the most glorious names of the Supreme God are given to Christ, and we can not therefore abandon our doctrine, without indorsing blasphemy, and without involving ourselves in the absurdity that God has *no name* by which he can be distinguished from his creatures. To meet this, we think it incumbent on our opponents to show, by the definition of blasphemy, that our objection does not lie, and that there is no absurdity as we state.

2d. The most glorious attributes of God are predicated of Christ, and we therefore can not reject his Divinity without involving ourselves in the absurdity, that God has *no attribute* by which he may be distinguished from his creatures; and we think our opponents can not ask us in fairness to adopt *their* belief, without showing that this is no absurdity at all.

3d. The most glorious works of God are ascribed to Christ, and we can not therefore give up the doctrine of his Godhead, without nullifying the *divine argument* by which the *existence* of the Almighty is proved; without involving ourselves in the absurdity that a creature is his own Creator, and that this creature-creator *may be and not be*, at the same time; and without involving ourselves in another no less, namely, that God has performed *no work* by which he may be distinguished from his creatures. We think that these must be met by arguments to prove them no absurdities at all.

4th. The worship of God by angels and men, by the inhabitants of heaven and earth, is represented as given to Christ; and we can not therefore but believe he is *God*, without involving ourselves in the absurdity, that God has no *peculiar worship* by which he may be distinguished from his creatures. This too must be shown to be no absurdity at all.

5th. We must believe that Christ is *God* as well as man, because if only man, he is the *worst man that ever lived.* We think this must be met, by showing that he being only a man, did not dissemble when on oath; that he made no false impressions upon the Jews; that he did not, by his omissions of statement, by his representations and inducements, lead men to *worship* him, and that he is not the object of the highest religious worship by the representation of the Revelation.

Now, we ask, have these arguments, presented in various forms a thousand times, ever been met? We have reason to believe they never have; certainly nothing has come within the range of our own observation but irrelevant texts, which only prove what we most fully admit. We most distinctly believe our

Saviour is man, having a human body and a human soul, both of which are necessary to form human nature; that as a man, he was sent into the world to "magnify the law and make it honorable," by suffering the punishment that law pronounced against transgressors, in behalf of those who were given him before the foundation of the world; by which sufferings he magnified the law, in declaring its righteousness and immutability, and made it honorable by rendering a full satisfaction to its righteous demands in the room of his people. This is a distinctive feature of our belief, which Dr. Channing calls the "heart-withering faith of the Genevan school!" But we also believe that Christ is the Supreme God; and we have given our reasons for it according to the direction in 1 Pet. 3 : 15.

An author already quoted says:* "Unitarians take the Bible in their hands, as they say, and sitting down to read it, as plain unlettered Christians, and with prayer for Divine illumination, they find that the general tenor of its language either distinctly asserts or necessarily implies the Supremacy of the Father, and teaches the inferior and derived nature of the Son. In proof of this, they appeal to such passages as the following: 'This is life eternal, that they might know thee, the only true God, and Jesus Christ whom thou hast sent.' (John 17 : 3.) 'For there is one God and one Mediator between God and man, the man Christ Jesus.' (1 Tim. 2 : 5.) 'My

* Rupp's History, p. 705.

Father is greater than I.' (John 14 : 28.) 'My doctrine is not mine, but his that sent me." (*Ibid.* 7 : 16.) 'I speak not of myself.' (*Ibid.* 14 : 10.) 'I can of mine own self do nothing.' (*Ibid.* 5 : 30.) 'The Father that dwelleth in me he doeth the works.' (*Ibid.* 14 : 10.) 'God hath made that same Jesus, whom you crucified, both Lord and Christ.' (Acts 2 : 36.) 'Him hath God exalted with his right hand to be a Prince and a Saviour.' (*Ibid.* 5 : 31.)"

Now, we solemnly believe that all these texts, and many more, "distinctly assert, or necessarily imply the Supremacy of the Father, and teach the inferior and derived nature of the Son," as to his humanity. This, therefore, forms no difference between us. To present that upon which we are *agreed*, as an argument in the matter upon which we *disagree*, is egregious trifling. These texts are in perfect harmony with those we have quoted in proof of the Supreme Godhead of Christ, upon the admission of his two natures; but upon the supposition that he is a mere creature, they are perfectly irreconcilable, the whole Bible becomes an enigma that must baffle every attempt at producing an agreement between these two classes of texts. We can show their harmony upon our doctrine; but without it, no such harmony, in our opinion, can be made to appear. To present these texts, then, being wholly irrelevant, is to no purpose. Why not take the texts which we think *prove* the Deity of Christ, from both the Old and New Testament, and cope with them? Why not "take the Bible in their hands, and sitting down to read it, as plain and unlettered Christians, and with prayer for Divine illumination," strive to show how Christ can be called Jehovah, the Most High God, the True God, the only Wise God, the Everlasting Father, the Great God, God over all, blessed for ever, Omniscient, Omnipotent, Omnipresent, Eternal, Immutable, Our Creator, Preserver, and final Judge; and yet, with all these most glorious perfections, be only a CREATURE? This would be achieving something to the purpose, it would be a rare piece of work, which the world as yet has never seen. Until this be done, there is no fair argument and no meeting of the *real* question in dispute at all.

But lest we might be thought reluctant to touch these texts, we will briefly consider them. Christ says in his prayer: "This is life eternal, that they might know thee the only true God, and Jesus Christ whom thou hast sent." Christ as *man* prays to God in the behalf of his chosen. As such he is manifestly distinguished from the Father. He was the "*sent* of God," who came to do his will. But does this text prove that Christ was not God? No, it only distinguishes the manhood of our Redeemer from the Godhead. If it prove that Christ is not the *only true God*, by the same reasoning the Father can be proved not to be the *only wise God*. Jude thus prays to *Christ:* "Now unto Him that is able to keep you from falling, and to present you faultless before the presence of his glory with exceeding joy, To the *only wise God,* our Saviour, etc." If the one text excludes the Son from Deity, the other must exclude the Father from Deity. But this writer exclaims: "Does a Being pray to himself?" We might answer this by asking: Does a Being *present to himself?* How can Christ present "us to himself, or before the presence of his glory?" If He be but a *man*, the last text involves the very absurdity complained of; but if he be God as well as man, the objection is answered: as man, like other men, he prayed to God, whose nature is as distinct from Christ's human nature, as from ours, but yet united with it in a way ours never can be. In some places the Scriptures speak of Christ as *God*, in others as *man*, and in others as *God and man*. In all this there is no contradiction.

1 Tim. 2 : 5.—For there is one God, and one Mediator between God and man, the man Jesus Christ."

Mediation implies *satisfaction*, and for this purpose it was necessary that our Saviour should be God and man, for how could a mere man satisfy God for his fellows? Besides, if Christ was only a *man* why is the statement to that effect made? Why the assurance, that *that man*, was a man? It must have been for one of two reasons, either to guard us from supposing he might be God or an angel, or to intimate that he was both God and man, the *man* being the mediator, because the sufferer by whom satisfaction was made. It could not have been to guard us against this supposition; for, in the next preceding verse but one, our Saviour is denominated *God;* therefore the intention of the Apostle must have been to point us to the specific nature in which mediation was made "by God our Saviour." This text therefore in its connection, is plump *against* the system in whose behalf it has been pressed.

John 14 : 28.—My Father is greater than I.

By urging this text our opponents not only make out that our Saviour was a man, but also, by consequence, that he was a *blasphemer!* These words contain a comparison, and for any creature to compare himself with his Creator, is arrogance, presumption, and blasphemy. Besides, it makes our Saviour talk nonsense! What would be said of the best man that ever lived, should he stand up among his fellows and say: "My Creator is greater than I am!"

A perusal of this chapter will show conclusively that Christ's comparison had no respect to *nature*, but to *work*. He describes himself as the great *ambassador* sent to our fallen world, and in this respect "the Father that dwelt in him doeth the works," and is therefore greater than He. So Christ as an *ambassador*, said: "I speak not of myself."—"I can of mine own self do nothing." Such language was perfectly suited to him in his *official* capacity. Thus we can clearly explain every passage of this nature in perfect consistency with our doctrine, and we are confident that a multitude of passages, some of which we have quoted, can not be tortured into consistency with the scheme of our opponents. We have given a sample of Unitarian exposition which speaks for itself. Let it be also observed, that the spirit of inspiration in John, by this scheme, is made inconsistent with itself; for in the first chapter of this gospel the Word that was made flesh, is asserted to be GOD; but if this text prove Christ to be nothing more than man, it also proves that John in the first chapter penned a falsehood!

The great objection made to our doctrine is this, Christ is everywhere styled the *Son of God*, and he calls God his *Father*. Now, as the Scriptures were given to us that we might understand them, as they speak to us in terms that we can comprehend, terms familiar to us, terms descriptive of human things and relations, when these are applied to divine things, it is argued, that the human relation of Father and Son, must necessarily suggest the inferiority of the Son to the Father when speaking of a divine relation.

As we have already considered this phrase, we must be very brief. Either it denotes identity of nature with God, or it does not. If it does, there is an end of the argument; if it does not, then it remains with our opponents to show how they can vindicate our blessed Saviour from prevarication. The Jews understood this phrase to denote equality with God, and Christ knew it; and without correcting their mistake, he died in the support of an untruth! Besides, the Apostle says: He "thought it not robbery to be *equal* with God." Now, when we compare this with the interpretation the Jews put upon his words, when we consider that the reason why they stoned him was—"that he being a man, made himself *equal* with God; because he said, *I am the Son of God*," we can see no way of escape from the belief that Christ is God. But why did he call himself the SON, using a term that conveys to us the idea of posteriority and inferiority? We reply, that we are bound so to interpret the phrase, that it will not contradict the explicit declarations of Scripture. This term expresses a distinction in the Godhead which we can not understand. The terms, *Father* and *Son*, with us denote *identity of nature;* but when applied to the Godhead it does not therefore follow, that the relation must be in *all respects* the same. When men, worms of the dust, begin to explain the mode of the divine subsistence, and erect their deductions of reason into a standard of faith, they act like the men who assert there is no bottom to the ocean, because their lines are too *short* to fathom it. "Who by searching can find out God?" We must be content with revealed *facts*, when they are above our finite capacities; but when we transcend this obvious duty, "our foolish hearts are darkened."

Thus we show how the texts Unitarians appeal to, are altogether wide of the matter in controversy. *They do not prove their negative.* They are entirely in harmony with our faith. But the proof-texts we offer, they can not make to harmonize with their system, without the torturing irons of a proudly pretending criticism, and without shameful reflections upon the sacred penmen, when their words are too obstinate for Unitarian management.

But we must not forget that our opponents are philosophers, and reasoners; for they often have "had great reasonings among themselves:" and they are metaphysicians, too; and they upbraid us because we are neither. Thus writes Dr. Channing:

"We believe Jesus is one mind, one soul, one being as truly one as we are, and equally distinct from the one God. We complain of the doctrine of the Trinity, that, not satisfied with making God three beings, it makes Jesus Christ two beings, and this introduces infinite confusion into our conceptions of his character. This corruption of Christianity, alike repugnant to common-sense and to the general strain of Scripture, is a remarkable proof of the power of a false philosophy in disfiguring the truth as it is in Jesus."

Again he says: "According to this doctrine, Jesus Christ, instead of being one mind, one conscious intelligent principle, whom we can understand, consists of two souls, two minds; the one divine, the other human; the one weak, the other Almighty; the one ignorant, the other omniscient. Now we maintain that this is to make two beings." "Can you conceive of two beings in the universe more distinct? We have always thought that one person was constituted and distinguished by one consciousness. The doctrine that one and the same person should have two distinct consciousnesses, two wills, two souls, infinitely different from each other, this we think an enormous tax on human credulity."

Here the Doctor professes to give our exact sentiments on this subject. Has he done so? NOT AT ALL. Who ever maintained the absurdity, he has presented? NO BODY. Who ever so taxed human credulity as to demand such a belief in Christ? NO BODY. Why then is this statement made? We know not, unless to display the skill of certain sporting gentlemen who set up *Nine Pins* to knock them down again. Now we believe as fully as any could wish, that the representation Dr. Channing has given is both unphilosophical and irrational. He either understood our views, or he did not. If he did not, this representation of them, charges him with ignorance with which a man of his acknowledged abilities can not be taxed. If he did, then it charges upon him something else.

Our view of the person of Christ, can not be more lucidly stated than in the language of Dr. Dick. "Christ is as truly man as he is God. This peculiar relation was indispensably necessary to the unity of the Mediator. Had the two natures, however intimately connected, not been personally united, their actions would not have been referable to one agent; there would have been two agents perfectly distinct, whereas, now, the person of Christ, if I may so express myself, is one principle of operation in the accomplishment of our redemption."

"To illustrate this point more fully, I remark, that it was *not a human person* which our Saviour assumed, but *a human nature.* The distinction between these is important, and should be carefully considered. By a person, we understand an intelligent being subsisting by himself, and not dependent upon any other. This is the meaning of the word when it is used in reference to men; when applied to the Trinity, it expresses a distinction which we can not explain. To say that the Son of God assumed a human person, would be an express contradiction, because there is an idea imported in the word assumed, with which the personality of his human nature is absolutely inconsistent; for it imports that he made it his own; and besides, on this supposition, as we have already remarked, the acts of the man would not have been the acts of the Son of God, and consequently, would not have been available for our salvation. He assumed a human nature, or, in other words, made it his own nature, by giving it a subsistence in his *divine person.* The term *personality* merely imports, that the nature of which we are speaking, subsists by itself. To deny, therefore, the personality of the human nature of Christ, takes nothing from it that is essential; it simply represents it as standing in a peculiar relation to another nature. It would have been a person, if it had not been united to the Son of God;

but, being united to him, it can not be called a person, because it does not subsist by itself, as other men do; each of whom has an independent existence."

"When in speaking upon this subject, we use the phrase, the constitution of the person of Christ, it is necessary to guard against a misapprehension of the meaning. It is not that his person is made up of two constituent parts, the divine and the human nature; for this would imply that the Son of God was not a person before the union or that he became a different person after it."*

We have been lengthy in our quotation, to show the utter unfairness of Dr. Channing's representation, and we can not avoid believing, that he very well knew the exact sentiment of this quotation, to be the faith of orthodox Christians. How far then he is to be trusted in his statements of the creed of others, is quite obvious. We believe that Christ was a perfect man, but as he was born unlike other men, so he subsisted unlike other men; and all this is perfectly compatible with reason and revelation. It avails nothing to cry down, as theory, what Dr. Dick has expressed so well, because it is irrational.

* This view is not peculiar to Dr. Dick. Long before his day, it was presented, and has been often and ably advocated, as the true state of the case respecting the constitution of our Mediator; argued out, from the necessity of presenting the basis, upon which the two classes of texts teaching a two-fold nature, are clearly harmonized. (Mark's Medulla, p. 186. De Moor, vol. iii., pp. 759, 760. Fisher's Catechism, p. 102. Calvin's Institutes, vol. i., p. 436.)

If we believe it to be true, because no other will harmonize the Scriptures on this question, it can only be expurgated from our faith, by showing that Unitarian faith harmonizes them as well, without impeaching the veracity and qualifications of the inspired writers.

Dr. Channing further states: there are "comparatively *few* passages, which are thought to make him (Christ) the Supreme God." Whether this be true, we leave to the judgment of the candid reader. But perhaps it may be a matter of curiosity to know how these few are managed by the most distinguished and able man who has appeared in this country, against the Deity of our Lord.

He says: "It is our duty to explain such texts by the rule which we apply to other texts, in which human beings are called gods, and are said to be partakers of the divine nature, to know and possess all things, and to be filled with all God's fullness. These latter passages we do not hesitate to modify and restrain and turn from their most obvious sense, because this sense is opposed to the known properties of the beings to whom they relate; and we maintain, that we adhere to the same principle, and use no greater latitude, in explaining as we do, the passages which are brought to support the Godhead of Christ."

But where do we find texts informing us that human beings are partakers of *the* divine nature? Nowhere. The single text alluded to, is 2 Pet. 1 : 4, where believers, it is said, by the promises may be partakers of *a* divine nature, clearly alluding to the new birth, the being born from above. Is "the most obvious sense" here the *divine essence?* Where are creatures said to "know all things"? Nowhere. Where are they said to "*possess*" all things? Nowhere. Is the phrase "that ye might be filled with all the fullness of God" in its "most obvious sense," "the fullness of the *Godhead*"? Certainly not. The former must mean the fullness of which God is the author, and which he imparts to his people; the latter, the fullness of his own essence. The immediate context of words and phrases is the place to look for the "most obvious sense" of a passage. The basis, therefore, of this rule, is simply the *assumption* of a parallelism between those passages, which support the divinity of Christ, and others containing similar words and phrases, whose context shows that no such parallelism exists.

If the Bible be the work of inspiration, if all its parts have the common impress of a Divine origin, nothing can be clearer than this, we must adopt that faith in which all its revealed facts shall harmonize. Upon the admission of the Godhead of our Redeemer, every passage respecting his person and his work is beautifully consistent with the whole; but if this be denied, then before any thing like consistency can be seen, we must take all the texts specifying the most glorious names, titles, attributes, works, and worship of the Deity, that are applied to Christ, and subject them to the operation of a rule, by which they must be MODIFIED, RESTRAINED, and TURNED FROM THEIR MOST OBVIOUS MEANING!!! What an admission! What desolation and destruction does this carry over the whole field of divine truth! Was there ever such a rule of *exegesis* as this, by which the Holy Oracles are made to bend to the preconceived opinions of men? What rule could better subserve the interest of the Papacy and of Deism? Let it be carried out, and we shall soon get rid of the Bible altogether, for it lays the groundwork for a DENIAL OF ALL REVELATION. To systems of faith, as well as to men, the words of Christ apply in all their force: "Wherefore, by their fruits shall ye know them."

The scheme that ignores the doctrine of the Supreme Godhead of Christ, denies also other vital doctrines of the Christian system, namely, atonement and satisfaction by Christ, the total depravity of our nature, regeneration, and justification by grace. On the other hand, it apologizes for human depravity, it makes good works the ground of deliverance from wrath, and of the enjoyment of heaven. It exhibits Christ as a man who came only to set us an example of virtue, by the imitation of which, we *work our passage* to a happy immortality. It denies the doctrine of endless punishment, holding that "no act of a finite being, a frail, sinning child of dust can possess a character of infinity, or merit an infinite punishment." According to it, the moral quality of sin can not lead to infinitely disastrous results, notwithstanding the Bible says: "Many of them that sleep in the dust of the earth shall awake, some to everlasting life, and some to shame and everlasting contempt." The wicked "shall go away into everlasting punishment; but the righteous into life eternal." "Is not thy wickedness great? and thy iniquities *infinite?*"

Unitarians deride the sentiment, that the finite act of finite man, can originate infinite evil; but this question (see Job. 22 : 3) strongly implies the affirmative. The history of our race proves that such is the fact. If God should please, there is nothing in the nature of things to prevent the continuance of our world and our race as they now are, *ad infinitum.* He made man pure and perfect. "By one man sin entered the world, and death by sin, so death has passed upon all, FOR that all have sinned." Whatever may be the explanation, here is taught (Rom. 5 : 12) a causal connection between the first sin and all human depravity; but this depravity, undeviating in its tendency, has run on for nearly six thousand years, and at this day its resultant evils are more numerous than ever. Hence sin is an infinite evil, because it has a self-perpetuating power. And as change of location can not produce change of character, the sinner, dying impenitent, goes on to sin for ever; and if the operation of the law of our being be the same in the next world as in this, and for aught we know it is, then and there it will beget progressive intensity of woe. Neither God, nor himself, nor any hallowing influence, will ever change his moral character; for Christ said to the Jews, "Ye shall die in your sins, and where I am ye *can not* come." Hence as the evil, *per se*, perpetuates itself, it must also perpetuate the moral relations of the lost in "everlasting punishment," and is therefore an infinite evil.

Unitarianism repudiates these doctrines, but if we are able to understand the meaning of language, all these doctrines denied, are the very ones to which the greatest prominence is given. The doctrine of the vicarious sufferings of Christ pervades the whole Bible, and if this be stricken out, its value to us as sinners is nothing; for then the sentence stands out in horrible distinctness: "The soul that sinneth, it shall die." "Cursed is every one that continueth not in all things that is written in the book of the law, to do them." The question, then, must for ever remain unanswered, "How shall man be just with God?" and the appalling assurance must be to us the pledge of unutterable despair, "Except your righteousness shall *exceed* the righteousness of the Scribes and Pharisees, ye shall, in NO CASE, enter the kingdom of heaven." If the righteousness of our exalted Redeemer can not avail for the covering of human guilt, who dare, after a life of the fairest earthly fame is spent, and the applause of the world be the tablet of his epitaph, who dare stand upon his own merits before his final Judge? Talk not of repentance, tears of blood can never obliterate the stains of moral guilt. Sorrow for sin can never purchase exemption from suffering for sin. Mercy can never be shown until justice be satisfied. Therefore, the death of Christ must avail in reconciling these attributes of an immutable God, for the extension of relief. Because Christ was "made sin for us, who knew no sin, that we might be made the righteousness of God in him," Paul could argue with a "therefore," that there is no condemnation to the believer. If this be not the scheme of divine love, whose convergent focal rays consumed every doubt in his heart, and lighted a flame of rapturous joy within him, under the influence of whose glow he indited his eighth chapter to the Romans, he reasoned most absurdly. "Who shall lay any thing to the charge of God's elect? It is God that justifieth. Who is he that *condemneth? It is Christ that died*, yea, rather that is risen again, who is even at the right hand of God, who also maketh intercession FOR us." These are passages that fill us with all the animations of hope, but if there be no positive connection between the "blood of the Lamb" and the redemption of the soul, our hope is extinguished, our despair is begun. If we must turn away from the doctrine of Christ's righteousness as the procuring cause of salvation, to the cheerless hope of an unassured acceptance in the face of a broken law unredressed, what can that promise us but the bitterness of disappointment? No, reader, if we are *ever* saved, it must be by the embrace of this truth, "*The blood of Jesus Christ cleanseth from all sin.*" (1 John 1 : 1.) And when all earthly ties are broken, and we are launched away from time, our characters must have been moulded by the operation of this truth, if when on the billows of Jordan, our hope, like Noah's dove sent forth, shall bring us back the olive-branch of peace.

Our personal salvation depends upon our reliance on Christ, as the God-Man Mediator. "Being *justified by his blood,* we shall be saved from wrath through him." "He gave himself FOR us that he might *redeem* us from all iniquity." "We are *redeemed,* not with corruptible things, but *with the precious blood* of Christ." The song of heaven is this, "Thou hast redeemed us to God by thy blood." Now, if the means of our acceptance with God, be the merits of Christ, and if his people be bought by his'blood, it is perfectly plain that if we reject him as he is set forth in these quotations, we must be undone for ever. "Therefore, we ought to give the more earnest heed to the things which we have heard, lest at any time we should let them slip. For if the word spoken by angels was steadfast, and every transgression and disobedience received a just recompense of reward; how shall we escape, if we neglect so great salvation."

CHAPTER X.

CONCLUSION.

Socinianism dangerous—Our view of atonement proved right—Grand means of salvation—" What must I do to be saved?" unanswered—Brief address to those who deny the Divinity of our Lord.

In the foregoing pages, we have not said all that might be said to prove the Divinity of our glorious Redeemer; but we think we have said enough to show, that the denial of this doctrine is attended with serious difficulties, and followed by alarming consequences. We hope nothing has escaped our pen harshly written, for while we do hold Socinianism to be a most dangerous perversion of the Gospel, we are conscious of nought but an earnest desire that they who are misled by it, may be brought to weigh it in the balance of Bible-truth. We think the Deity and atonement of Christ are so explicitly laid down in Scripture, that nothing but a desire to maintain a party, could determine any mind to do violence to the word of God, in order to evade their admission. If it be necessary, in the interpretation of those passages that clearly prove these doctrines, to "modify, and restrain, and turn from their obvious sense," the words of the Holy Ghost, what reliance can be placed upon the Bible at all? If the licentiousness of criticism be allowed to change the meaning of words and phrases, does not this at once carry ruin to our Rule of Faith? Does not the system which avows such a principle, betray itself as the perversion of the Gospel?

If God's love was manifested simply in the gift of a *man*, whose duty was to inform us that He will save on our repentance; and to present us an example which we must follow; what higher exhibition of love did He give in this bestowment, than in sending that "cloud of witnesses" Paul mentions, whose virtues and patience in suffering, taught precisely the same lesson, and were designed for the same effect? By such a view of the transcendent love of God, we think this text, and others of like import, denuded of their peculiar preciousness, and made to convey an impoverished sense, wholly unworthy of their language, and far below their obvious import. The sufferings of Christ, are held up as the great attractions of the Cross; and the atonement for sin which they effected, thus delivering from a righteous condemnation all those who by faith repose in Him for victory over sin, death, and hell, is made the great theme of the New Testament. "*He appeared to put away sin by the sacrifice of himself.*" "*Who his own self bare our sins in his own body on the tree.*" "*For Christ also hath once suffered for sins, the just for the unjust, that he might bring us to*

God." "*Blotting out the handwriting of ordinances which was against us, nailing it to his cross.*" These texts, beyond a doubt, teach the doctrine of vicarious suffering. If not, what do they teach? If they do, then what can engage my soul more than a view of Christ sustaining the pains of death, that my salvation might be attainable? What can so melt down my hardness as a view of the Royal Sufferer laying down his life to save me from the curse of the law? But if he died as the mere victim of human violence, if there were no more virtue in his blood than in the blood of a martyr, how are these texts to be vindicated from falsehood and deception?

The Gospel presents the *atonement* of Christ as the broad basis of our hope, and the grand means of salvation. Hence Paul says: "I endure all things for the elect's sake, that they also may obtain *the salvation which is in Christ Jesus* with eternal life." But if Jesus did nothing for our salvation, but preach a future state, establish right principles of conduct, and present a holy example for our imitation, we ask how is salvation *in* him more than in any other man who did the same things?

By the scheme which strips Christ of his Godhead, the whole Bible, we think, is stripped of its interest to us as sinners; for, if he be only a creature, it is impossible to receive the doctrine of atonement by satisfaction. The declaration that *God will by no means clear the guilty*, stands out in fearful prominence, and when we turn to the fruits of our own defective obedience, as the reasons for our acceptance with God, we are met with the assurance, "*By the deeds of the law there shall no flesh be justified in his sight.*" This text, and many others, imply that we MUST BE JUSTIFIED from the guilt of sin, that is, *constituted just* before God. But if this can not be done, either by the righteousness of Christ imputed to us, or by our own works, then the question remains unsolved by Unitarian Christianity, "What must I do to be saved?" If we be told, we must "believe on Christ," we ask what is there peculiar in him upon which our faith can fasten? WHY is this direction given? What *connection* is there between an act of simple intelligence, and the salvation of the soul? We can see none. But viewing Christ as our "Passover slain for us," we have an important reason to offer, why he is to us "the chief among ten thousand," and worthy of all our love. We regard him as our "SURETY," "*Whom God hath set forth to be a propitiation through faith in his blood—that He might be just, and the justifier of him who believeth in Jesus.*" Without this Suretyship of Christ, we believe we CAN NOT BE SAVED, and we think this is strongly made out by Divine argument.

We hope it may be taken kindly, by those of our readers who deny the doctrine advocated in the foregoing pages, if we briefly lay before them the consequences, which we think inevitably follow the adoption of Socinian sentiments. We think this our duty, and it is difficult to discharge it faithfully, because it is no easy matter to convince an opponent of honest purpose and sincere friendship manifested in an attempt to overthrow his principles, to expose to himself his errors, and delineate their results. He thinks thereby either his intellect or his heart, or both, are really impeached by such an attempt, and therefore is apt to retire within the strongest fortress of prejudice. We therefore protest in the outset, against any imputation of this kind; we profess and possess honesty of purpose, and sincerity of friendship, in our most earnest entreaty to be impartially and candidly heard. Men of great minds and generous impulses, have professed the distinguishing doctrine of Unitarianism; but he has much yet to learn of human nature, who supposes that in the matter of religion, especially, greatness of intellect or amiableness of disposition, will guard the soul from delusion, or save from the fatal effect of deplorable mistake.

Confessedly, you who deny and we who hold to the divinity of Christ may be equally sincere, and therefore may debate this question without calling down fire from heaven on each other. We have staked our all upon the respective systems herein presented, each claiming to be *the truth* relative to the most important point in Christian theology—most important, not only in itself, but because of the vital doctrines which stand or fall with it—most important because our characters in the estimation of our Judge are good or bad in his sight, according to the *faith* that forms them. *Social* virtues can never take the place of *religious* ones in this or any other respect. The *morality* prescribed in the *second* table of the law can not compensate for the want of the morality prescribed by the *first.* *Man looketh upon the outward appearance, but the Lord looketh upon the heart. As a man thinketh in his heart, so is he. He that believeth on the Son hath everlasting life; and he that believeth not the Son, shall not see life, but the wrath of God abideth on him.* These words of Scripture show the falsity of a favorite sentiment often in the mouths of men: "He can not be wrong, whose life is in the right."

Were the mere interests of sect or theory alone involved in the previous discussion, we should not have taxed your attention with what we have written. But far beyond this, the SALVATION OF THE SOUL is the great matter involved. Upon no question ought we to expend more serious and anxious thought than this, *What shall it profit a man, if he gain the whole world and lose his own soul?* What is meant by losing the soul, is plain from the words of Scripture, or there is nothing plain under the sun. *The wicked shall be turned into hell, and all the nations that forget God.* This is a clear threatening of banishment from Him. To make "Hell" here, to mean the grave or the invisible state of the dead, is absurd; because the *good* shall be turned into both. Christ has given us the meaning we must attach to this phrase.

Mat. 10 : 33.—*Fear not them which* KILL *the* BODY, *but are not able to kill the soul; but rather fear him who is able to* DESTROY *both* SOUL *and body in* HELL. 25 : 46.—*These shall go away into* EVERLASTING PUNISHMENT, *but the righteous into* LIFE ETERNAL.

Now, supposing we are mistaken as to the meaning of these and similar passages, and that in the end, it shall turn out that we have been providing against dangers that have no existence. What then? Shall we be worse off for this? Upon your own principles, we shall not. It shall be well with us, and it shall appear even in the case of perfidious Judas, that *it is better for him that he was born*, notwithstanding the high authority that decided otherwise.

But upon the supposition that you are mistaken, in the interpretation of these passages in your denial of endless banishment from God, what then? Christ said: *If ye believe not that I am he ye shall die in your sins, and where I am ye can not come.* This is plain. He who dies in his sins, dies unforgiven, unredeemed, unpurified, and enters the future world precisely in the same character with which he left this. What then?

Rev. 21 : 27.—*And there shall in no wise enter into it* (heaven) *any thing that defileth, neither whatsoever worketh abomination, or maketh a lie.*

Now, if we do not resort to Dr. Channing's rule for twisting texts, it certainly appears that the bulk of probabilities is in favor of our interpretation, and that the mass of argument is against that of the Universalist and the Unitarian. If we are mistaken, it is of little consequence; but if you are mistaken, the consequences are awful. If Christ be God, those who reject his divinity and expiatory sacrifice, can never come where he is, and this consideration is our apology for our plain speaking. We have studied *both* sides of this controversy, and we think it our imperative duty to state, what we think we have proved, *the truth.* Faith has a controlling agency in the formation of Christian character; for the want of a certain kind of faith, is THE reason for the assurance given, *where I am ye can not come.* If our premises and conclusions be incorrect, it is of little consequence; but if they are, as we hold them, true—then we think the whole matter is summed up in this syllogism:

Whoever finally rejects any of the claims of Christ, can never be where he is.

But Supreme Divinity is a claim of Christ; therefore

Whoever finally rejects the Supreme Divinity of Christ, can never be where he is.

This is the great claim He made, and in the support of which he died. If Christ be not God, it is impossible to accept the doctrines of "Orthodoxy;" therefore, the distinctive formative faith just spoken of, depends upon this leading claim of our Redeemer. We wish to state painful truth, without exciting prejudice, and without giving offense. The interest involved is too great to allow us to be deterred, by any apprehension of what they may say, whose first interest is to uphold a system. And we can not apologize for the solemn truth stated by Christ himself.

The possibility of any ground for this argument, commends it to earnest attention. The proofs of Christ's divine nature we have given. We think they can not be met by proofs of his human nature, about which there is no dispute. It appears evident, that Unitarians must fairly get rid of the dilemmas in which they are placed, before they can consistently denounce us as *uncharitable*, for framing the syllogism we present for your consideration. The *major* is based upon the strong declaration of Christ; the *minor* is based upon the general argument of this book, whose particulars, with their consequences, we have carefully studied, and confidently submit. The *conclusion* is based upon reason, of which it has often been said we are sadly deficient.

This tremendous consequence, therefore, should lead us to banish every extraneous question, every "side-issue," and settle it with ourselves whether it be wise, safe, or even generous towards our own souls, to neglect or reject this doctrine for which we contend, on the ground of alleged "intrinsic impossibility"—an *à priori* assertion, which may be confronted with the declaration of Paul: *The wisdom of this world is foolishness with God.*

Now, then, to what does the denial of the Divinity of Christ lead?

1. It leads to a degradation of the Scriptures. We

have given extracts from the book of a convert from "Orthodoxy," entitled, "How I became a Unitarian." They are sufficiently startling, and show HOW. He began by degrading the word of God, before he could extort its aid in degrading the Son of God. He says, (p. 36:) "That the apostles were not men of an infallible judgment," (referring to what he is pleased to suppose their mistake as to the Lord's second coming,) "and that they could be mistaken upon a subject of the most engrossing interest to themselves and to the age in which they lived." And to show this, he exhibits Peter, "as possibly distrusting his own interpretation of the event, *ingeniously* qualifying the prediction, by saying that 'a day with the Lord is as a thousand years!'" Speaking of the character of Jesus, he says, (p. 104:) "It is only in a moral aspect that this character preserves, to our view of it, its beautiful consistency and striking heroism. And yet would this be sadly broken and disfigured, if we admitted much to be true that the Evangelists said of him. But this we can not do"!!! Once men get to this point, it is easy for them to answer every hard argument by denying the capacity or the inspiration of the sacred writers, or by adopting Dr. Channing's rule of "turning texts from their most obvious meaning." When we follow such guides, it is a great kindness if Providence send a voice to whisper in our ears, "Beware of the ditch!"

2. It leads to a denial of vicarious atonement by

the blood of Christ. We have quoted a few passages which corroborate that emphatic one, "*Who his own self bare our sins in his own body on the tree;*" and we might fill pages with extracts from the Scriptures to the same purpose. Now, if Christ be not God, Unitarians are quite consistent in rejecting the atonement, because it is absurd to suppose, that the most perfect man that ever lived could "by any means redeem his brother" from the power of sin, or from the curse of the law. But we are told, *without the shedding of blood there is no remission. The blood of Jesus Christ cleanseth from all sin. He made peace through the blood of his cross. The blood of Christ shall purge your conscience from dead works, to serve the living God.* The song of the redeemed is: *Unto him that loved us, and washed us from our sins in his own blood. Thou art worthy to take the book*, etc.—*for thou wast slain, and hast redeemed us to God by thy blood out of every kindred, and tongue, and people, and nation.* These and many more texts make the doctrine of vicarious suffering as plain as words can make it. There is salvation in no other way to any man who rejects it. (Acts 4 : 12 ; 1 Cor. 15 : 3; Eph. 2 : 14–16 ; 1 Pet. 4 : 1; Heb. 2 : 2, 3.) This is clear, from what Paul says, (Rom. 5 : 8, 9, 11 :) *But God commendeth his love towards us, in that while we were yet sinners Christ died for us. Much more then being now justified by his blood, we shall be saved from wrath through him—by whom we have received the atonement.*

In opposition to this, the author last quoted says,

(p. 116:) "No theological fiction can save him (the sinner) from the moral stain with which his sin taints him, and the *only atonement*" (italics our own) "he can make to the moral law, is to wash it out with his tears (!) Then God can forgive as well without as with the merits of another." We really believe that no *fiction* can save any body from any thing; certainly not from being tainted with a moral stain! Nor do we think that any such washing is required by God, or competent to man, because impossible in the nature of things. Further, we think that "the only atonement" here allowed, upon which God can forgive, is no atonement at all, nor can all the tears ever shed, cancel moral guilt. Man can make no atonement for his sin of any kind. He may *receive* atonement by Christ, but nowhere in the New Testament is he required to *make* atonement, simply because it is out of his power. (Jer. 2 : 22.) *For though thou wash thee with nitre, and take thee much soap, yet thine iniquity is marked before me, saith the Lord God.*

Seeking salvation by the merit of Christ, he says, (p. 117,) "would indict the believer as seeking the appropriation to himself of another's virtues under 'false pretenses.'" A very extraordinary indictment, indeed! We can very well understand how one may appropriate to himself the *benefits* of another's virtue, as in the case of suretyship; but "to seek to appropriate another's virtue under false pretenses," is a most remarkable seeking! While these rare specimens, not of "English pure and undefiled," but of the author's *strong* views of things in a *new* light, are impartially compared with the Apostle's words, it seems to us, conviction must flash upon the candid mind, that Unitarianism, as it is called, is a *perversion* of the Gospel, which goes to subvert a man in the cause of his own salvation. If the Bible be true, it can not be otherwise; for our tears and our doings, it is asserted, will gain more for us than the blood and righteousness of Christ! But He has taught in language that admits of no mistake, and which should make Unitarians tremble, because, by their own showing, it was spoken of Unitarians: *Except your righteousness exceed the righteousness of the Scribes and Pharisees, ye shall in* NO CASE *enter the kingdom of heaven.*

We are frequently reminded that the *Jews* were all *Unitarians.* The men alluded to by our Saviour in the last quotation, stoned him because he made himself *equal* with God, saying that God was his own Father. They were therefore zealous Unitarians, rejecting the *sacrifice* of Christ as the procuring cause of reconciliation with God, and contending for salvation by works. Indeed, aside from their national customs, they were, as to faith, very little different from Unitarians of the present day, than whom, however, they were far more consistent; because, rejecting the claim to divinity which Christ made, they took him to be a very bad man, on that account; and the more dangerous, because of unim-

8

peachable character, thereby beguiling the common people, who, not seeing his ulterior aim, took him to be a good man, and, if we may judge from numerous examples, regarded and worshipped him as divine. Now, if Christ could thus affirm of the zealous Unitarians who crucified him, what shall be said differently of those of the present day, whose religious faith and dependence were in all respects the same as theirs, but without the advantage of their consistency? It seems very plain, then, that *Unitarian righteousness* shall in NO CASE procure admission into heaven. Unless Christ be *made unto us wisdom, and righteousness, and sanctification, and redemption*, there is nothing left to us but a *fearful looking for of wrath.* God *hath made him sin for us, who knew no sin; that we might be made the righteousness of God in him.*

Because your salvation entirely depends upon the satisfaction and righteousness of Christ, which the Unitarian system repudiates, we say to you, Beware of Unitarianism. It will wrap your soul in the winding-sheet of the second death. Say not, this is uncharitable. It is the very reverse. For if it be an act of kindness to drag a man in sweet repose, from his bed, around which the flame is curling; if it be kindness to probe the agonizing victim of disease, to save his life; then it is kindness to cry aloud and spare not, *lest the cross of Christ be made of none effect*, in the estimation of men taught to regard Him, simply for example's sake, as the sublime hero of a tragic tale.

It is our hope, dear reader, that our company has not been unprofitable. If you have been benefited, we are satisfied; but before we part, in view of what Christ has done for us, let us join in saying:

"TO THE ONLY WISE GOD OUR SAVIOUR BE GLORY AND MAJESTY, DOMINION AND POWER, BOTH NOW AND EVER. AMEN."

DEAR dying Lamb, thy precious blood
Shall never lose its power,
Till all the ransomed Church of God
Be saved to sin no more.

E'er since by faith, I saw the stream
Thy flowing wounds supply,
Redeeming love has been my theme,
And shall be till I die.

Then in a nobler, sweeter song,
I'll sing thy power to save,
When this poor lisping, stammering tongue
Lies silent in the grave.

Lord, I believe thou hast prepared,
Unworthy though I be,
For me a blood-bought free reward,
A golden harp for me!

'Tis strung, and tuned, for endless years,
And formed by power divine,
To sound in God the Father's ears
No other name but thine.

COWPER.

APPENDIX.

In his controversy with Dr. Priestley, Bishop Horsley gave the substance of the following letter, to show how easily Mohammedanism and the scheme of Dr. P. might be made to amalgamate. This letter was written more than a century before, and although by his own showing its sentiments were his own, Dr. P. roundly denied its authenticity; whereupon the Bishop had recourse to the original document, which he found in the Archiepiscopal Library at Lambeth, written in a very fair hand, with two other papers on the same subject; and he thus writes: "I do most solemnly aver that I have this day, Jan. 15, 1789, compared the letter to Ameth Ben Ameth, as published by Dr. Leslie in his *Socinian Controversy Discussed*, with the manuscript in the Archbishop's Library, and find that the printed copy, with the exception of some trivial typographical errors, is exactly conformable to the manuscript, without the omission or addition of a single word."*

This letter was rejected by the Mussulman without examination; thus it came to be preserved in the said Library. We transfer it from Leslie's works, now scarce, as a *theological curi-*

* Horsley's Tracts, p. 270.

osity, mainly interesting on account of the practical tendencies and exegetical manifestation of the system it advocates—a system in no respects altered since the fraternal overture was made to the followers of the False Prophet.

AN EPISTLE DEDICATORY TO HIS ILLUSTRIOUS EXCELLENCY

AMETH BEN AMETH,

Embassador of the mighty Emperor of Fez and Morocco, to Charles II., King of Great Britain.

Amongst the many splendid entertainments and receptions, amidst the several congratulatory encomiums and presents, that were offered unto your excellency, as public testimonies of the esteem and admiration the inhabitants of this Western Empire do justly conceive of the mighty and glorious Emperor of Morocco, your master, and of your own peculiar virtues, there hath been no such address or present made unto your excellency, none, as we presume, that was of a weightier importance (though slenderer appearance) than this which we now submit to your liking and acceptance at your departure. For the contents thereof, being about the mysteries of that all-sufficient and invisible one Deity, its own intrinsic value needs no words, nor the usual adornments that might be expected from us, to set it out with an outward splendor to so discerning a person in spiritual and sublime matters as your excellency is known to be, even in the judgment of learned universities. Besides, truth in these countries is fain to go sometimes, like princes, in a disguise, who, being out of their own kingdoms, are driven to put by their royal habiliments, for to converse with more safety and freedom with a few wise and faithful worthies they can best trust. Religion, then, excellent sir, the religion of an *one only Godhead*, (as also of many other great verities wherein ye agree with our sect, and disagree from *other* Christians,) is the veiled princess, whereof we are now become the venturesome ushers into your excellency's presence; I said venturesome, not by reason of any affront we need fear at your hands, but rather from the rash severity of some of our own fellow-Christians here, for venting those verities we *shall declare to hold in common with you*, (which are contrary to them;) yet Christ's and our spirit is otherwise, to essay by gentle persuasions and *union* with all mankind, as far as may be.

Know, therefore, noble sir, that we are of that sect of Christians that are called Unitarians, who, first of all, do, both in our own names and in that of a multitude of our persuasion, (a wise and religious sort of people,) heartily salute and congratulate your excellency, and all that are with you, *as votaries and fellow-worshippers of that sole supreme* Deity of the Almighty Father and Creator. And we greatly rejoice, and thank his divine bounty, that hath preserved your Emperor and his people in the excellent knowledge of that truth, touching the belief of an only Sovereign God, (who hath no distinction or plurality of persons,) and in many other wholesome doctrines wherein ye persevere, about which this, our western part of the world, are declined into several errors, from the integrity of their predecessors. But besides this much in the general, our attendance on your excellency at this time hath a more special prospect, as you shall perceive by the sequel. For about thirty or more years, there came an embassador, as your excellency is, from the Emperor of Morocco, into Europe, with whom Count Maurice, of Nassau, Prince of Orange, (a Protestant Christian,) and the Prince of Portugal, (a Papal Christian,) held a conference about the Christian and Mohammedan religion. The embassador deferred then to speak fully his mind on the matter till after his return home; and when he had there consulted with the learned in the Alcoran, he sends his answer in a letter which not only sets forth the tenets of his own religion, but also refutes some errors held among the Protestant and *Romanist*

Christians, in some of which, as in other points, we presume, that embassador was mistaken and misinstructed. Now we herewith present unto your excellency a faithful transcript of that letter, that's with difficulty to be seen, only in the cabinets of those princes to whom it was directed in Latin; not that we account the contents thereof to be a novelty to you that are of that religion, but because it is a piece of rarity and learning; and chiefly for that it is the foundation on which we build another small piece or two in the same language; the which we here dedicate likewise unto your Emperor, to your excellency, and to his Mauritanian subjects, the which comprehends the main design of our waiting on you at present. Now, forasmuch as that noble embassador doth in this letter write some things which to us seem very ungrounded, and therein charges without sufficient distinction the whole body of Christians with such errors which we *Unitarians* do abhor as well as the *Mohammedans*, with whom *we must agree* in such, even against our *other* fellow-Christians; therefore we that are fain to be more exercised soldiers in such controverted points of religion, and should best know the differences in Europe about the same, shall undertake in this, our second and third treatise, (which are but as observations on that letter,) first, to set forth, (for your better information,) briefly and distinctly, in what points all Christians do generally agree with the *Mohammedans* in matters of religion; secondly, in what things Christians universally disagree from you, with the reasons for the same; thirdly, in what cases you do justly dissent from the Roman Catholics; fourthly, that Protestant Christians do join with you in your condemning of those *Romish* errors, and theirs and our reasons for the same; fifthly, we intend there to lay down in what articles we, the *Unitarian* Christians, (of all others,) *do solely concur with you Mohammedans*, (to which we draw nigher in those important points than all other Protestant or Papal Christians.) With our additional arguments to yours, to prove that both *we and you* have unavoidable grounds, from Scripture and reason, to dissent from other Christians in such verities, (though we do count them otherwise,) our brethren in our Lord Jesus Christ.

Therefore, in the sixth place, we, *as your nearest fellow-champions for those truths;* we, who, with our *Unitarian* brethren, were in all ages exercised to *defend with our pens the faith of one Supreme God,* (*without personalities or pluralities,*) *as he hath raised your Mohammed to do the same with the sword, as a scourge on those idolizing Christians;* we, I say, in this, our peculiar lot in religious controversies, shall, in our duty of love, undertake to discover unto you, in these our books, those weak places that are found in the platform of your religion, and shall herein (with your favor) offer to your consideration some materials to repair them; for we do (*for the vindication of your Law-Maker's* glory) strive to prove that such faults and irregularities, not *cohering with the fashion of the rest of the Alcoran building, nor with the undoubted sayings of your prophet, nor with the Gospel of Christ,* (whereof *Mohammed* would have himself to be but a preacher,) that therefore (I say) those contradictions were *foisted* into the scattered papers found after Mohammed's death, of which, in truth, the *Alcoran* was made up, it being otherwise impossible that a man of that judgment, that hath proved itself in other things so conspicuously, should be guilty of so many and frequent repugnancies as are to be seen in those writings and laws that are now a days given out under his name. We do, then, in these our papers endeavor to clear by whom, and in what time, such alterations were made in the first setting-out of the *Alcoran;* and though we have ten times more to urge on the same subject than we present, yet by a few summary touches that we have here in a few days made up for your view, we suppose there may be enough to satisfy any unprejudiced and thinking persons. Such as it is, we beseech you to accept thereof as friendly advices left to your reason and conscience to judge of with yourselves, seeing we offer not the same as to defame or upbraid you, but out of humanity and a loving spirit, to the end that, if you think fit to examine and redress those errors, we may by your proceedings *stop the mouths* of your adversaries, against whom we are often fain *to stand for you* in such points wherein we may well and reasonably do it. Lest, after all, your excellency should judge of this our undertaking and present in a narrow and contracted idea, suitable to the slenderness of our persons, parts, or retinue, who are but two single philosophers,* and yet come as orators of those *Unitarians* whom we proclaimed to be so great and considerable a people, it is necessary we should give a short view of the antiquity and extent of this noble sect, and hint to you the reasons that make them in these European parts use such cautiousness, and as to their sentiments to carry themselves, as those princes I mentioned, to go *incognito.*

As to their antiquity, I need but call it to your mind that not only all the patriarchs down from Adam till Moses, not only all the Jews under the written Law and the Old Testament, to this very day, were still worshippers of an one only God, (without a trinity of persons,) but that also all the primitive Christians, in and after Christ and his apostles' time, never owned any other besides that single and Supreme Deity; and all the true and purest Christians, their lawful disciples, do to this very day worship no other but the sole Sovereign God, the Father and Maker of all things. And therefore are we called *Unitarians*, as worshippers of that one only Godhead in essence and person, that we may be distinguished from those backsliding Christians named *Trinitarians*, who own three coëqual and self-subsisting Persons, whereof every one is an absolute and infinite God, (as they pretend;) and yet they'll have all these three to be

* The agent of the Socinians who bore this letter was Monsieur Verze. As they would have expurgated the Koran, so they have the New Testament; and all traces of the divinity of our Saviour are expunged in their Improved Version. This was easily done by the aid of Criticism, and of Dr. Channing's rule.

but one God, which is such a contradicting absurdity, that certainly our wise Maker and Lawgiver would never impose it to be believed upon that harmonious and relative rectitude he hath placed in the reason of man. But of the first who opposed this rising error in old times was Paul of Samosate, a zealous and learned Bishop of Antioch, with his people and adherents; he lived sixty years before the Council of Nice, that was held on this subject about three hundred years after the ascension of Christ our Lord. There was also Marcellus, Bishop of Ancyra, in Galatia, with his friends and followers; Eustathius, Bishop of Antioch, and Arius, a Presbyter of Alexandria, with many more that lived in the time of that Council, did openly withstand and refute the *Trinitarian* schism, as we see in the chronicles of that age. I omit Photinus, Bishop of Syrmium, and the famous Nestorius, with many more persecuted persons for the same truth, who, though they had some nominal differency about the two curious expositions of those mysteries, yet they agreed in that main point of the undistinguished sovereign unity. And from the reign of the Emperor Constantine, both the oriental and occidental Empire generally persisted for some hundred years in that same faith, resisting those contradictory opinions of the Trinitarians. Even in the declining times of Christianity, occasioned by the growth, or the tyrannical usurpation, of the popes and clergy, who would force their private notions and human inventions on men's consciences; that is, in the reign of the Emperor Charles the Great, about the year 800, Bonosius and Elipandus, with other bishops and Christians in Spain, unanimously opposed the doctrine of the Trinity. And of late years, in Europe, stood up the pious and noble personage *Faustus Socinus*, and his *Polonian* association of learned personages, that writ many volumes against that and other sprung-up errors among Christians. But now, to lay before your excellency the extent of this orthodox faith of the Unitarian Christians, in what nations is it held, be pleased to observe that all the Christians throughout Persia, Armenia, Mesopotamia, those called of St. Thomas, and some Hollanders, and Portugese in Asia, those that live among the Greeks in Europe, even your neighboring Christians in Nubia—all those together (which far exceed the Trinity-asserting Christians) do maintain with us that faith of one Sovereign God, one only in person and essence.* *And why should I forget to add you Mohammedans, who also consent with us in the belief and worship of an one only Supreme Deity?* To whom be glory for ever. Amen.

But in the west and north of Europe we are not so numerous, by reason of the inhumanity of the clergy, who, contrary to the gentle ways of Christ, would convince us and others, but by fire, and thunder, and gaols, and swords of princes, though our patient carriage and brotherly love towards them for their precious truths we still hold in common, might evidence to them of what sort of spirit both they and we are. Yet our people are numerous in Poland, in Hungary, Holland as well as England; but being under the threats of such un-Christian persecutors, (which hath been, in the wisdom of God, the lot of all true Christians from the beginning, for to try, exercise, and fortify their knowledge and virtue by the opposition of their adversaries,) we can not open ourselves, nor argue touching our faith, but that even our nearest friends that are Trinitarians, out of a mistaken zeal, would be the first to deliver us up to bishops' courts, prisons, and inquisitions, to the endangering both our lives and fortunes. That is the sad reason that we have not hitherto *waited in greater numbers to congratulate and welcome your excellency*, nor can at this present in such a manner as we well judge to be suitable to your grandeur, and the *respect we bear to your prince and people*, for any share of divine truth you or any other do hold entire with us from our God and from our Saviour Christ.

Countenance, therefore, this philosophical plainness and freedom, (that's part of our profession,) which embolden us two to be more

* Bishop Horsley has sufficiently invalidated these claims.

forward than others of our persuasion to offer to you, rather than fail, even a mess of our own trade, such slight presents in appearance as those little books are, whose contents, nevertheless, we think so important for the good of your souls that we would be ready (if acceptable) to go and assert the contents thereof to the learned of your country, *had we any prospect of success*, while we are uncertain what *entertainment* attends such as would object any thing against your Alcoran, be it never so modestly and lovingly proposed.

Therefore, since we can not now in person, be pleased, noble sir, to communicate the import of these manuscripts to the consideration of the fittest persons of your countrymen, only as a scantling of what the more learned of our Unitarian brethren could say, far beyond any thing that's here on these subjects of our differences. And lest you might think it too mean an office to be instrumental in spreading any such divine verity, consider, if it be so great a matter to perform the part of an embassador among earthly princes, (which your excellency hath so laudably done of late,) how far more glorious is it to undertake the least embassy in the cause and religion of the Supreme Monarch of the world? To whom be glory and dominion for ever. Amen.

INDEX.

www.ingramcontent.com/pod-product-compliance
Lightning Source LLC
LaVergne TN
LVHW011227110826
845150LV00006B/1566